The Cosmic Sting:

Truth Revisited

by

Randolph Hammer

DORRANCE PUBLISHING CO., INC.
PITTSBURGH, PENNSYLVANIA 15222

For information or to order additional books, please write:
Dorrance Publishing Co., Inc.
643 Smithfield Street
Pittsburgh, Pennsylvania 15222
U.S.A.
1-800-788-7654
Or visit our web site and on-line catalog at *www.dorrancepublishing.com*

This book is lovingly dedicated to every individual who discovers truth leading to membership in God's eternal family.

Contents

Introduction

Why write another book about such a controversial subject? Millions of books have already been written. Who could possibly be interested in another? Especially since there can be no definitive answers to such imponderable questions. Or can there be?

The thousands of religious and philosophical ideas that have been propounded seem confusing and contradictory. With so much contradiction and confusion, how could any one system of belief hold a conclusive and meaningful answer? Is truth in the spiritual realm really unattainable? Is there any way to wade through all the confusion to find true reality?

Are there no solid meaningful answers? Answers that could bring deeper meaning into one's inner personal world? Answers that would bring harmony to the bewildering and often agonizing struggle of everyday life? Answers that conclusively deal with our fearfulness and uncertainty about life after death?

This writer could accurately be described as a reluctant author. This is not a book I wanted to write. Seeing the uncertainty and confusion in the world market of ideas, philosophies, and belief systems was simply too compelling. Truth was too compelling!

Truth, if it is obtainable, holds ironclad answers—answers that involve startling resolutions—for all those who are willing to be open and utterly honest with themselves. Those who are not afraid of change and of developing new frontiers of living. Those who are willing to expose their most cherished beliefs to truth and are ready to discard them if necessary. To get their lives on track with reality.

I sincerely believe that, through the process of simple logic, truth is within reach of every living soul. Truth that will bring a new and transforming level of reality to all honest seekers.

Chapter One
What is Truth?

The implications of truth can be frightening! Especially in the future tense. No one is immune from the consequences of truth. Every living being is paving a private road to eternity on the basis of moment by moment, seemingly insignificant choices. It rarely occurs to us how incredibly strategic each choice is. Each choice we make has a powerful relationship to truth, and the sum of these choices is inexorably building our future. Not only in this world, but in the world to come!

Truth is defined as, "That which conforms with fact and reality; exact accordance with that which was, is, and will be." It has dimensions in the past, the present, and the future. It is a three dimensional chronological continuum.

Common examples of truth are to be found in the physical laws of the universe. We have observed their performance in the past and the present. These observations give us assurance of their same consistent performance for the future. Truth is a predictable constant. It can always be relied upon to produce the same results. The day to day operation of our very civilization is dependent upon these physical constants.

Science has demonstrated through various means of measurement that our physical world is based upon laws which have demonstrable reality. Some good examples are found in the force of gravity, the constant weight of various physical sub-

1

stances, the speed of light and sound, the earth's rotation, mathematical tables, and innumerable others. The world of reasoning minds has readily accepted the truth of these physical laws and their daily dependability. They stand unquestioned. It must be remembered, however, that scientific learning is limited to only two dimensions of truth. The past and the present. Science has made tremendous strides in the development of our modern civilization. Mankind has given a nearly all-encompassing acceptance to the scientific method. This acquiescence to science may possibly have blinded many to its limitations. Science is limited to the realms of the measurable. Therefore science is limited to the realms of the past and the present. It cannot speak with authority in the realms of the future.

Unfortunately, many have come to feel that science has all the answers. That the unmeasurable is non-existent.

There is another dimension in the world of humanity. The emotional-spiritual dimension. The non-physical aspect of human personality. The scientifically unmeasurable dimension. The dimension that asks questions like, Where did I come from? Why am I here? What is my purpose? Where am I going when I die? Is there a God? Is He knowable, if He exists? Perhaps due to the fact that our human minds are limited to observations of past and present only, it seems we have been left to "grasp at straws" for solid answers to our future. A future that most certainly involves physical death. And consequent uncertainty.

The prevailing view of many seems to reject any possibility of objective spiritual truth. Truth that includes the future dimension. Is it within the realm of possibility that spiritual truth could be objective and verifiable? Are there spiritual laws in existence that are as immutable as the physical laws upon which our universe is founded? Laws that include a future dimension?

It will be readily acknowledged that the natural human mind is limited to the discovery of truth in only two of its dimensions. The past and the present. This accounts for the voluminous attempts by human thinkers to invent belief systems that promise a rosy picture of the future for their adherents. We have occasionally been amused by these prophets and seers. Many have managed to hoodwink large numbers of followers into embracing their predictions—claims sometimes pinpointing a doomsday target date at some future time. We may have seen these doomsdays come and go and the consequent unraveling of the seer's credibility. We have discovered that the human mind is limited to the realms of past and present truth exclusively.

It must be acknowledged in the light of these facts that any belief system that could demonstrate future dimensional truth consistently and accurately must be supernatural in origin, especially if this future dimensional truth was verifiable over a period of hundreds, even thousands, of years. Among all the documents and belief systems in existence, none can demonstrate future dimensional supernatural truth. Except one! The Judeo-Christian Bible.

The three dimensional aspect of truth has tremendous implications for every system of belief that claims supernatural truth. Supposed truth. Proposed by human thinkers. Every honest, thinking person must face this fact, especially if he or she has committed to one of them. This test of truth must be applied to every belief system that propounds spiritual truth. Then it must be discarded as error or accepted as truth. The capacity to demonstrate consistent, accurate future dimensional truth is proof positive of any system's origin. Such truth separates fact from fantasy. Such truth validates the supernatural origin of Christianity.

Here then is a simple and eminently logical test—a test that can easily be applied to any system of supposed truth. Any thinking person can cut through the myriad religions and philosophies simply by applying this truth test: Does the system reveal truth in all three of its dimensions? Any system that cannot meet this standard can be discarded as purely human invention, unworthy of further serious commitment or consideration. These belief systems can make no valid claims regarding the future or the afterlife. They can be no more valid than the reaches of human imagination. Their failure to demonstrate the future dimension of truth invalidates their claims to be supernatural. Do not make the mistake of committing your eternity to such a "leaky vessel." Truth will not deviate to accommodate error. Christianity alone among all the religions and belief systems in the world presents spiritual truth. In all three dimensions, as we will discover.

Chapter Two
Reality of the Unmeasurable

A number of years ago, while traveling in Canada, this writer spent a few days in Banff. Banff is steeped in an overpowering atmosphere of startling magnificence. Lush, green mountain meadows are rimmed with overpowering rocky mountains towering high above the valley. My appetite suggested it was time for the evening meal. Since I happened to be walking on the campus of the local university, the thought of taking the evening meal there was appealing. Upon entering the cafeteria, it was apparent to me that all the tables were taken. There was one large table occupied by two young men. They appeared to be very cordial. When asked about the possibility of sharing their table, they responded favorably. As we ate, they related the occasion of their presence in Banff. Their permanent homes were in the eastern United States. They were both Ph.D. physicists attending a summer seminar for promising young scientists in their field. Following our meal, they invited me to take a walk in the woods with them. As we walked alongside a lovely stream, I felt compelled to share my Christian faith with these brilliant young scientists.

While relating my life-changing experience, one of them smiled and affirmed his approval. The other reacted in a clearly negative manner. He stated that he was a scientist and was committed to the physical realities of the scientific method. He went on to say, "If you could show me the footprint of this God you describe, I could apply the scientific method and prove His existence." He pointed to a large, deep, well-defined footprint in the soft soil of the trail on which we were walking. "Since you can show me no physical, demonstrable proof that he exists, I cannot accept the possibility of his existence."

I asked him if he were married. He affirmed that he was. I then asked him if he loved his wife. He responded that he loved her very much. I stated, "I am sorry, but I cannot believe that you love your wife unless you can show me physical, demonstrable proof of that love. If you could show me a footprint of your love in the soil of this trail, then I could apply the scientific method and believe in the existence of that love of which you speak."

I pointed out that we as human beings are essentially a human spirit encased in a human body. We regularly experience an entire spectrum of feelings which are scientifically unmeasurable—feelings such as love, hate, anger, jealousy, resentment, despair, envy, and many others. Feelings that are common to all members of the human race. Although we can feel the results of these powerful emotions, they do not yield to the test tube. They are invisible and unmeasurable. They exist only in the emotional-spiritual realms of our existence. They are devoid of physical parameters.

Since we possess a human spirit without measurable physical dimensions, it is inconsistent and illogical to reject the possible existence of God, a supreme creator who is also scientifically unmeasurable. We, as spiritual beings, behold a physical world which we perceive through the processes of our own unmeasurable human spirits. If we deny the possible existence of an unmeasurable God, then common logic demands that we deny the existence of our very own unmeasurable human spirits.

The young scientist had subscribed to the common error of some in the scientific community. Those who tend to believe that the unmeasurable is non-existent. They fail to consider their own unmeasurable human spirits and the reality of the unmeasurable dimensions that comprise the unseen personal

6

world. The mode of their own emotional lives. The lives they function with every day. This young man left with a greatly changed view of God's existence.

The Bible unequivocally declares that God created mankind in His own image. He created us with the capacity to experience a personal world which includes many powerful emotions. Emotions that are both unmeasurable and invisible. Just as God is. Wonder of wonders, God clearly chose to design within each individual the capacity to know Him as a friend and helper through the complex spectrum of our inner personal world. The difficulty we have in coming to know Him may very well exist in our failure to perceive accurately the unmeasurable nature of our own human spirits. Perhaps we should consider the fallibility in some of our individual perceptions. And in doing so remain open to the reality of unmeasurable truth. Truth that may usher us into an entirely new and revolutionary way of life. Truth that includes a startling future dimension.

Chapter Three
The Cosmic Sting

The principle of future dimensional truth conclusively demonstrates the fact that the Bible is a supernatural book. There has never been another document comparable to it in the entire history of the human race. How then can we account for the fact that only a fraction of the world's population has responded to its message? The message that God, the creator of all things, deeply loves every individual in the entire human race. That all mankind could now enjoy an entirely new personal world. A personal world characterized by love, joy, and peace. Why would any thinking person, recognizing the reality of truth in its three dimensions, reject such an unspeakably wonderful proposition for their lives?

One obvious answer to this question is the fact that large blocs of divergent cultures in the world have not yet had a clear and understandable presentation of biblical truth in everyday terms they can understand. Other cultures have had cultural-religious traditions for centuries—traditions that have little or no tolerance for the proclamation of the Bible message in their lands. The Christian message has, however, been proclaimed in most of the world's cultures, especially in the Western world. The Western world has often been described as presently experiencing a post-Christian era. Nations that were formerly characterized by vast majorities of active, practicing Christians seem to have largely departed the faith. If the Bible alone can demonstrate its divine origin, why are so few committing to its message?

The Bible contains the answer to this seemingly imponderable question. Here is the unwelcome truth. There is an incredibly powerful, invisible, deceptive, cosmic being. A being sworn to the eternal destruction of all mankind. The soul of every individual on the face of the earth. A being who is somehow able to penetrate every aspect of our personal human consciousness and every facet of our daily lives. Satan is somehow able to derail God's best plan for the lives of individuals, making his plan seem more rewarding than that of God's. Satan is so successful in his deception that he is able to blind nearly all of mankind to all the tragic consequences of self-indulgence. His plan seems wonderfully fulfilling to untold millions the world over. People do not indulge themselves unwillingly in sexual immorality, graft, corruption, alcohol and drug abuse. These activities seem so self-fulfilling. Rewarding. Enjoyable. Yet future dimensional truth results in personal debilitation and misery for those who engage in them. Not only in this lifetime, but in the unseen lifetime ahead. In eternity.

Satan is the driving force behind these self-destructive actions of men and women. They are diametrically opposed to God's best intentions for us. They can only lead to moral wreckage, destroyed relationships, sorrow, and regret. We will discover that the Bible is the Book of Truth, that the God of the Bible is the God of Truth, and that Jesus Christ is the Man of Truth.

Let us examine some supporting evidence from this remarkable document. From the teaching of Jesus Christ evidence clearly establishes the fact of the cosmic sting. Jesus related this startling record of Satan's pre-eminent place in the destruction of mankind's souls.

Matthew, Mark, and Luke all record Jesus' parable of the sower. The importance of this parable is underscored by its threefold appearance in the New Testament. Jesus said:

> "A sower went out to sow his seed; and as he sowed,
> some fell by the wayside; and it was trodden down,

and the fowls of the air devoured it. And some fell upon a rock; and as soon as it was sprung up, it withered away, because it lacked moisture. And some fell among thorns; and the thorns sprang up with it, and choked it. And other fell on good ground, and sprang up, and bore fruit a hundred-fold. And when he had said these things, he cried, He that hath ears to hear, let him hear. And his disciples asked him, saying, What might this parable be? And he said...Now the parable is this: The seed is the word of God. Those by the wayside are they that hear; then cometh the devil, and taketh away the word out of their hearts, lest they should believe and be saved. They on the rock are they who, when they hear, receive the word with joy; and these have no root, who for a while believe, and in time of testing fall away. And that which fell among thorns are they who, when they have heard, go forth, and are choked with cares and riches and pleasures of this life, and bring no fruit to perfection. But that on the good ground are they who, in an honest and good heart, having heard the word, keep it, and bring forth fruit with patience."[1]

The basis of Israel's economic survival was largely agricultural. Jesus therefore used illustrations that were in the language of the people. They had observed the various conditions of the soils they planted each spring. They had seen the seed which had been spilled by the roadsides and pathways and its subsequent loss to birds. The seed had been unable to begin its cycle of growth. Rocky areas offered only temporary sustenance, resulting in short-term survival. The thorny soil offered nutrients sufficient to maintain life for the seed, but the thorns' sheer volume left the grain with no value to the farmer. The good soil, on the other hand, produced bountiful, healthy crops.

Jesus was setting forth the four basic conditions of the human heart. Every individual on the face of the earth falls into one of these four categories. Every individual will respond to the Word of God in one of these four ways. The seed illustrates the tremendous potential of life-changing reality in response to God's Word—its ability to bring forth new life, bringing spiritual nourishment and health to each individual's personal world depending on the type of soil they are.

Jesus makes it eminently clear who the conspirator is. The one who blocks a heart response that would result in new life. It's Satan. He prevents the Word from penetrating the heart, as illustrated by the roadside soil. This is an authoritative statement on the condition of various human hearts. A statement that leaves not the slightest margin of doubt. Jesus clearly establishes the fact that all who reject the message of the Gospel are victims of Satan's conspiracy. Satan's sting operation is the most devastating program anyone will ever face in an entire lifetime. The tragedy of it is that it's so cleverly devised and deceptive. The one who is victimized never sees the reality of his or her eternal destruction until it is too late to escape it. The effectiveness of Satan's deception is clearly illustrated by Jesus. He tells us that the vast majority of the human race is being swept unknowingly into Satan's evil web. In his Sermon on the Mount, Jesus states, "Enter in at the narrow gate; for wide is the gate, and broad is the way that leadeth to destruction, and many there be who go in that way; because narrow is the gate, and hard is the way, which leadeth unto life, and few there be that find it."[2]

Jesus' message is clear and unequivocal. Satan has somehow surreptitiously managed to invade our personal worlds. We have all been lied to via his penetration of our innermost perceptions. His unique ability to infiltrate our view of truth has us believing that there are no objective absolutes.

We have come to feel that truth is unrelated to spiritual issues. To each his or her own views, we believe. It doesn't matter what you believe, so long as you're sincere. All those who fall in this category have been successfully tolled into the cosmic sting. Such individuals have been led into an irreversible eventual membership in Satan's tragic community of ruined,

remorseful souls. Can those who have fallen into this trap extri-
cate themselves before it's too late? An honest examination of
truth is the answer. Our greatest weapon against Satan's wiles is
truth. Truth alone will expose his evil program.

God's eternal purpose has somehow mysteriously permitted
both Satan and mankind to have complete freedom of choice for
a limited time, until the time of physical death. God has given
Satan frightening powers to infiltrate the consciousness of men
and women the world over. Satan is described in the New
Testament as:

"The Prince of the power of the air."[3]
"The spirit that works in the disobedient."[4]
"The foe of Christians."[5]
"The ruler of darkness in this world."[6]
"The source of spiritual wickedness."[7]
"Influencing the imaginations."[8]
"The god of this age."[9]
"The king of death."[10]
"The prince of this world."[11]
"The deceiver."[12]
"Beelzebub (prince of demons)."[13]
"The wicked one."[14]
"The tempter."[15]
"A liar."[16]
"A murderer."[17]
"The enemy."[18]
"An angel of light."[19]

Many other descriptions of Satan are to be found in God's
Word, all delineating Satan's great power and consummately evil
nature. Let us review the fundamentals of any successful sting
operation. The basic motivation driving any sting operation is
illegal gain, which is so cleverly disguised that the victim is totally unaware of the entire process until it is too late for recovery.
The deception must be so cleverly planned that the victim is
blind to the entire process. Until after the conclusion of it.

God, as the creator of mankind, has an eternal love for every member of His creation. He longs for every individual in His creation to experience His love, joy, and peace. For every individual personally to know and enjoy Him throughout eternity. Satan, as God's sworn enemy, is committed to sabotaging God's fulfilling design for mankind. The human individual is God's most precious created resource. A personage designed with all the potential to experience God in a deeply personal way.

For Satan to thwart God's program for humanity seems to be his major purpose on earth. To steal from God myriad individuals to populate his own community. To somehow demonstrate to God that he, Satan, is wise enough and powerful enough to derail God's loving purpose for all. To blind humanity to its existence. To lead individuals off into an eternity of remorseful misery. Having fallen into Satan's trap of deception. Irreversible deception! Eternal deception! Blinding deception!

Chapter Four
The Blinding Process

The apostle Paul, in his letter to the Corinthians, makes this remarkable statement: "But if our Gospel (good news) be hidden it is hidden to them that are lost, in whom the God of this age (Satan) hath blinded the minds of them who believe not, lest the light of the glorious gospel of Christ, who is the image of God, should shine unto them."[1]

These words of the great apostle harmonize precisely with Jesus' parable of the sower. He makes it clear that those who reject the Gospel have been deceived by Satan. Blinded to the truth. In addition to God's direct and specific message in the Bible, God has chosen to communicate in another way. Through the somewhat mysterious medium of transmitting thoughts to our conscious minds. In some respects much like the media method of transmitting messages through the airways via radio and television. Some Christians refer to these as convictions—convictions that somehow become powerful forces, bringing about new spiritual insights. Insights often resulting in dramatically changed views of life. Insights that change the ways these individuals relate to others. Change them for the better.

Now here is the startling thing! God has inexplicably chosen to give Satan equal air time. He too can transmit thoughts into our heads! Our mental receivers function loud and clear. With Satan's messages! Simply look into your own secret thought life

14

for any single given week. What if this secret thought life could be captured on videotape? How about this idea? How willing would you be to have an audience view this videotape? The audience would contain every friend, peer worker, and family member. Be honest with yourself now! The creator God of this universe, and of you, is constantly viewing that video of your secret thought life. He doesn't need the videotape. Is that an unnerving thought for you? It should be. Because our thought life is where we live in reality. It's not what other people see. It's the real you!

The Bible tells us that God is constantly searching the hearts of men and women the world over.[2] Satan is described in the Bible as "the tempter." Many of the temptations that enter your thought life were authored by Satan. They are not all necessarily your own. The key issue is what you choose to do with these destructive thoughts. It's your decision that determines their result.

Our media reports every imaginable type of heinous crime committed every day. By the thousands. Each of these horrible crimes originated in the minds of the criminals. God was not the author of them. Satan was. The perpetrator embellished the original temptation until he or she chose to act it out physically.

There seems to be a nearly universal scorn for the concept of a supernatural, evil, cosmic personage. One who has the desire and the resources to insert evil influences in the private personal worlds of individuals. Those who present this concept are seen often as religious fanatics. Crackpots!

The teaching of history's most authoritative man clearly contradicts this view. Jesus Christ never once questioned Satan's existence. On the contrary, Jesus depicts Satan as a living super-natural being. A being with personality. With supernatural com-munication skills. With awesome, unthinkable power over the entire world of humanity. He even goes so far as to offer all the kingdoms of the world to Jesus if Jesus will only worship him instead of God.

Throughout the Gospel narratives he is seen again and again to be utterly and frighteningly real. To be invariably involved in the promotion of evil. That includes you! And me!

The New Testament is replete with illustrations of Satanic activity in the lives of innumerable individuals. He is seen as having the ability to disrupt both the physical and mental health of many, to plant evil thought patterns in the mind—patterns that often result in destructive acts.

Jesus was teaching in a synagogue where he met a woman. She had been oppressed by a spirit of infirmity for eighteen years. She is described as, "Bowed together and unable to lift herself up." Jesus called her to him and "loosed her from her infirmity," by laying his hands on her. She was immediately able to straighten up. The ruler of the synagogue was indignant because Jesus healed her on the Sabbath. Jesus rebuked him. "Ought not this woman, being a daughter of Abraham, whom Satan hath bound, lo, these eighteen years, be loosed from this bond on the Sabbath day?"[3] Modern day intellectuals would possibly scoff at this account. They may dismiss Jesus' analysis as mere superstition endemic to that day and culture. A modern physician might diagnose this as a case of osteo-arthritis. Many today feel that modern medicine has long since surpassed Jesus' knowledge of human ailments. Future dimensional truth conclusively establishes the fact of Jesus' divine nature, as we will discover in coming chapters. He created all things. According to the Bible. The Book of Truth. If he created all things, then he knows more than modern medicine purveyors.

Remember! Spiritual truth does not yield to the test tube. This dimension of reality is unmeasurable. Jesus' statements set the standard of truth. We tend to accept the medical names tacked onto human ailments as purely physical conditions. We don't even consider the possibility that these physical conditions may have spiritual causes that have promoted them.

Could Satan have that kind of power? Jesus says so. He says that Satan is the driving force behind many physical and mental infirmities. This doesn't necessarily imply that Satanic activity is the cause of every disease, but that possibility may certainly exist in some cases.

Another case of Satan-induced illness is documented. Jesus, in response to a deeply grieved father's plea, healed his son. A mute! Plagued by self-destructive acts. Throwing himself into the fire. Into deep water. Attempting to drown himself. Jesus commanded the evil spirit to come out of the lad. He was convulsed and lay as dead. Then he was restored to normalcy. The onlookers were both frightened and shocked, then delighted and awed at the power Jesus demonstrated. By mere words! Nothing more. The words of Jesus.[4] The Man of Truth.

There are many other instances of healings that were spiritual in nature. Mary Magdalene, a woman of ill repute, was healed of seven demons. Her life was later restored from a life of evil to a life of good. She experienced an entirely new level of living. Satanic forces had somehow penetrated her conscious mind, resulting in uncontrollable immorality. Satan has that ability. Jesus has the ability and the desire to reverse such self-destructive behavior.

During the first days of the early church a couple named Ananias and Saphira became pawns of Satan. They lied about a gift they had made to the church. The apostle Peter said, "Ananias, why hath Satan filled thine heart to lie to the Holy Spirit?"[6] Both husband and wife forfeited their lives as a result of having acted on Satan' temptation.

In another instance of Satanic deception, the apostle Peter was deceived.[7] When Jesus was foretelling his own death, Satan somehow infiltrated Peter's thoughts and motivated Peter to deny that it would happen. Jesus rebuked Peter with these words: "Get thee behind me Satan. Thou art an offense to me, for thou savorest not the things that are of God, but those that are of men." Satan's continued desire to undermine Peter's faith is seen also in a later incident in his life. Jesus said to him, "Simon (Peter), Simon, behold Satan hath desired to have you that he may sift you as wheat." Peter, subsequently acting on Satan's suggestion, denied Christ three times on the same day.[8]

In an additional instance of Satan's ability to communicate with individuals, he entered Judas's thought life, encouraging him to betray Jesus.[9] "Then entered Satan into Judas, surnamed Iscariot, being of the number of the twelve. And he went his way and conferred with the chief priests and captains, how he might betray him unto them."

There are many other instances of Satan's power displayed in the Bible. They present an alarming but accurate picture of Satanic deception by infiltrating the private personal world of various individuals' thought lives. His purpose never seems to vary. To blind, deceive, disrupt, derail, and destroy God's program. His program of restoration and love for every person on the face of the earth.

The Bible describes Satan as the prince of the power of the air.[10] The air is a medium with physical characteristics that perfectly promote the transmission of communication. Radio and television stations transmit through the air. Satan has a cosmic transmitter. We each have a finely-tuned receiver tuned to Satan's frequency. We don't need to tune in. We get Satan's broadcasts involuntarily. It's what we do with them that counts. Our responses determine the course of our lives. We make the decisions that determine our fate. Our lives are made up of these small, seemingly insignificant choices. Choices that God will never violate. God gifted each of us with a free will. He will never violate it.

To those who are physically blind, the realities of the physical world are entirely invisible. Unexpected objects are invisible, impossible for a blind person to detect. This inability to see physical objects can result in great personal injury or death. Satan has the plan and the power to perpetuate this same blindness on a spiritual level. Keeping us vulnerable to his deception for an entire lifetime. Leaving us without hope in eternity.

Jesus said, "I am the resurrection and the life; he that believeth in me, though he were dead, yet shall he live. And whosoever liveth and believeth in me shall never die."11 No leader in all the annals of history ever made such an all-encompassing statement. The goal of wise men and kings throughout the history of all mankind has been to find the secret to eternal life. None ever found it except those who have responded to the invitation of Jesus Christ. Only God could make such a promise. The wonder of responding to this invitation is that along with the response comes an inner certainty, an immovable assurance that you have found truth. Immediately when the commitment is made God sends the gift of His Holy Spirit to dwell in the new believer. The Holy Spirit's ministry includes the inner assurance that the gift of eternal life is a certainty. Jesus died to save us from a life of bondage. Spiritual bondage. Now God will accept us. Adopt us into His own family. Love us. Fill our lives with beauty. With love for others.

Satan doesn't want you to see truth. That's why he majors in the art of personal spiritual blinding to the existence of his personal presence in our private worlds, undermining our thought lives. Remaining invisible may be one of his most effective tools. Invisible and undetected. That's why so many people don't recognize or identify the source of many self-destructive thoughts that enter their heads. Thoughts that cause them to reject God's truth. Thoughts that trivialize the whole idea of Satan. The whole idea of a supernatural being with their eternal destruction as his main goal. A being capable of penetrating their private world in the realms of the imagination.

Chapter Five
Satan's Methodology

These are some of the specific avenues Satan employs to attain his nefarious goals in human lives.

CULTURAL FACTORS

Most of today's modern societies reflect a clear contrast between elements of good and evil in their midst. A substantial majority of the masses in most nations are basically law-abiding in nature, at least in their external conduct. This majority is in stark contrast to the minority of lawless citizens. Individuals whose lawless deeds are continuously the focus of the media. This contrast carries a tacit message to the majority. "I'm a good person. I don't commit crimes against persons or property." This kind of subconscious self-talk communicates a sense of moral well-being. Even non-violent crimes involving financial or political dishonesty are often reported in the media. Most of us are not engaged in these kinds of high-profile crimes. The contrast between our personal lives and these types of crimes simply accelerates our process of self-exoneration to personally acceptable levels. Thus the very fabric of our culture tends to perpetuate the underlying feeling that we're okay.

Most of us have done occasional good deeds. We may have helped an old person across the street. Given money to a homeless person. Remembered an anniversary gift. Visited the sick or imprisoned. Helped a needy friend. Let a helpless trapped motorist into our line of traffic. Started a diet or exercise program. Resisted criticizing our spouse for an obvious mistake. Lent a sympathetic ear to someone undergoing great stress. Most of us refrain from selling illegal substances.

The list goes on and on. These elements in our thoughts tend to make us feel that we are basically good people when we compare ourselves to the lawless elements in our society. The contrasts make this seem true. We reason, if we're a good person in this world, we'll be okay in the world to come. This universal kind of self-deception enables us to justify non-involvement in a program of life-changing dimensions demanded by true Christianity. This socio-cultural sense of well-being seems so right. It becomes a rut from which it is nearly impossible to break out—a rut that perpetuates spiritual deadness to the Christian message of abundant life. The Bible describes this condition of spiritual apathy: "There is a way that seemeth right unto a man, but the end thereof are the ways of death."[1] Our way seems right. It's not! It leads to eternal separation from God. Don't let deceptive cultural self-talk determine your eternity.

ORGANIZATIONAL MEMBERSHIPS

The mere fact of being a member in good standing in an organization that claims to assure eternal life for its members can be tragically deceptive. It is far more comfortable to turn over to some organization the responsibility for our eternal well-being. Then we don't have to deal with God on a one-to-one basis ourselves. Jesus gives a stern warning to such individuals. He tells us in no uncertain terms that we must take personal responsibility for our relationship with God. He said to the multitudes, "When you see a cloud rising in the west, you say at once, a shower is coming, and so it happens. And when you see the south wind blowing, you say, there will be scorching heat; and it happens. You hypocrites! You know how to interpret the appearance of earth and sky; but why do you not know how to interpret the present time? And why do you not judge for yourselves what is right."[2] Both the religious leaders and the common people were in the habit of making their own personal interpretations for their daily lives. In contrast to this personal function, for everyday life, they had shut down their own thinking processes in the spiritual department of their lives. They had shut down their hearts and minds to God on an individual basis and comfortably consigned their relationship with God over to their religious leaders or to the doctrines of their particular sect. These leaders claimed superior knowledge and judgment based on their status and religious training. Many had allowed their religious affiliation to become an opiate, blinding them to their individual responsibility to develop a personal relationship with God. One-on-one. From the heart.

Millions hold memberships in churches, societies, and organizations throughout the world. Most of these organizations have good moral standards. The members are generally required at least tacitly to accept these standards as a part of their joining ritual. There is often a cohesive sense of belonging that goes along with the joining process. An underlying feeling that seems to say, "I'm okay with God now. I've acknowledged these good moral doctrines. Never mind getting too radical in my religious life. I'll let the organization handle everything religious for me." That's a cop-out. No organization or church, no matter how well meaning, no matter how doctrinally correct, can do it for you.

This is precisely the attitude at which Jesus lashed out. He's saying that people will think for themselves in nearly every department of their lives. But not in the most important one of all: their personal, private relationship with God. We'd rather let the organization do it. That's easier. We don't have to face our own failures or change our ways of relating to others. Those who fall into this category have become victims of the cosmic sting. Blinded to the realities of truth.

LIFESTYLE FACTORS

When God created the human race, he created every individual in His own image to some extent. God, as a righteous creator, gave every individual a conscience. An innate knowledge about right and wrong. Even those without any kind of religious commitment have had a conscience at one point or another in their lives. Many do not heed it. Continual exposure to a broad spectrum of daily experiences can greatly desensitize it. Dysfunctional families resulting in childhood abuse. Peer groups espousing negative moral values. Media forces continually assaulting our minds, assaulting our moral standards with values that exalt self-indulgence. Materialism. Violence. Immorality. Deeply compelling forces. Forces that can slowly erode that inner awareness of right and wrong. Especially when choices are made that knowingly violate the conscience. Again and again. We have all participated in wrong choices at some time or another in our lives.

Individuals who are involved with an immoral or dishonest lifestyle can easily be turned away, dismissing instantly any serious consideration of a commitment that would involve change. Change in their value system that condones their present lifestyle. Those who embrace such lifestyles greatly diminish their consciences by doing so. A damaged conscience will readily convince one that forfeiture of their lifestyle would be an unacceptable alternative. Satan's blinding techniques capitalize in this area. Deception has triumphed. There is little hope for such individuals. Their eternity looks bleak apart from God's mercy and grace in Jesus Christ.

One of the marvels of God's goodness is His ability to change the desires of individuals who seriously commit to Him. Worldly pleasures once indulged in begin to lose their luster. Strange, new, and wonderful desires begin to emerge. The former focus of self-centeredness begins to give way to these new desires. Longings to reach out and to help others, to express God's love to others daily. Former pleasures that often left feelings of emptiness are transformed into deeply rewarding activities—activities that would have held little or no fascination prior to life-change elements. Elements that involve coming to know and love God as friend and helper.

If you feel threatened by this chapter, if you have a strong compulsion to reject the Christian message as a result of lifestyle factors you are countenancing, you should recognize this. You're being lied to. Subconsciously. By Satan. This is one of his major techniques to block you from making a commitment to truth— a commitment that will effectively thwart Satan's plan for your life. He's got you targeted, and he's zeroing in on you. He wants you for eternity. Thousands, even millions are falling into this trap. Daily. All over the world. Don't join them. Think truth. In its future dimension. Where is your life going?

IF GOD IS GOOD, WHY IS THERE SO MUCH EVIL IN THE WORLD?

Another effective technique used by Satan is this age-old question. Many will look at the overwhelming volume of evil in the world. In their minds, this is proof that a powerful, sovereign God does not exist. If He did, he would never permit so much evil. This view overlooks the entire subject of free will.

God created mankind with the potential of knowing and loving Him. Mankind was created to be a lover and a friend of God. He purposed that every individual should know, love, and enjoy Him throughout eternity. The opportunity of whether or not to love God could only be based on free will. The ability to make a free choice. If God had not created us with a free will, we would have had no choice. No option. We could have only performed in the way that God had programmed us.

Had He programmed us to love Him, we would have done so. But not by choice. The very nature of love demands free choice. No individual with a free will can ever be forced to love a partic-ular person. Love comes by choice. How would we categorize a creator who programmed his human creations to love Him? With no other option. He would be a manipulator.

We occasionally see individuals who try to make a particular person love them. Stalkers fall into this category. We feel sorry for them. They have chosen to focus their love on one who chooses not to love them. This kind of relationship can have no rewards for the one who is disinterested, nor for the manipulator.

Persons who become manipulators of others, who maintain a secret agenda for those they are attempting to manipulate, are only to be pitied. Their efforts are doomed to failure. They will only result in alienation and unhappiness for both parties. If God were constantly stepping into circumstances in order to manipulate the free choices of those who were making wrong choices, we would all simply be puppets.

No one would wish to have a God like that. Every thinking person desires the freedom to make their own choices, not to be controlled by others—much less by a sovereign being. We feel sorry for the masses who live in totally controlled societies under totalitarian governments.

That's why God gave every person in the world a free will. He will never violate it. But He will hold us accountable in the Judgment Day for every wrong choice we have made in our lives. We feel frustrated when we see bad people apparently get away with their evil deeds. We can take comfort from the fact that they will not get off scot-free. Their time of reckoning is absolutely certain. God has promised it will happen. That time is coming for everyone. That's why each of us is in such desperate need of forgiveness. The forgiveness only Jesus Christ can offer. The forgiveness that will put us right with God.

People choose evil rather than good. As they exercise their gift of free will. That's why we see so much evil in the world. The world would neither want nor accept a God who was constantly interfering, manipulating, and controlling the behavior of every individual on earth.

Much of the difficulty involved in making wrong choices that result in so much evil in the world is brought about by Satan. His ability to make self-destructive behavior so attractive and compelling. The Bible describes Satan as an angel of light.[3] What could be more appealing than an angel of light? And the styles of behavior such a supernatural being could present to the thought life?

The desire for unlimited material wealth. Sensual and sensuous euphoria encompassing the entire state of consciousness. Those who have overwhelming desires for immediate gratification rarely consider the consequences. The bank robber only visualizes the pleasures of spending large sums of money on self-gratifying kinds of things. Not the potential misery of personal injury or death. Not the ongoing agony of prison.

Controlled substance abuse is not engaged in because of the drudgery. Rather, it's because these substances offer a rush of euphoria. A temporary escape from unpleasant reality. No thought is given to the long-term consequences that may result. Prostitution. Robbery. Loss of self-respect. Loss of family. Prison. Suicide. Addiction that always grows into a greater and greater form of bondage.

Illicit sexual liaisons seem greatly to be desired. They are not entered into because they are uninteresting and uninviting. The immediate self-gratification has its own rewards. But the consequences are not considered before it's too late. The disintegration of families. Manipulation of people only for their bodies. Loss of self-respect. Sexually transmitted diseases. Potential early death. All are in the offing.

These things are prime demonstrations of Satan's crafty deceit in appearing as an angel of light. Penetrating each of our private worlds with tremendously appealing thoughts. Thoughts that seem incredibly desirable, nearly impossible to resist. Even if we want to resist.

Satan is simply reproducing his own rebellion against God in us. We want to be our own God. Call our own shots. Do what we want to do. The problem is God never designed us to be our own Gods. That's why we end up living such unrewarding lives so much of the time. He designed us to love and enjoy Him. To live not for self, but for others. Living by His design includes an abundant and fulfilling lifestyle.

TOO MANY PHONY CHRISTIANS

Many have rejected the faith as a result of watching professing Christians in the way they conduct their daily lives. Some seem to be living a hypocritical farce, blatantly contradicting the basic principles of the faith. Most have had some exposure to the tel-evangelist scandals of recent years. We have seen the self-serv-ing motives they have espoused and the millions they have deceived. We need to be reminded of this fact again: God has granted a free will to each and every human being.

We have all made wrong choices in our lives. We have all practiced deceit at one time or another. We have all been hypo-critical to some degree. Satan's cosmic sting has touched every one of our lives. God designed us to undergo a maturing process as we age. Most develop a degree of wisdom. Understanding. Consideration of others. Generosity. Kindness.

Hopefully this growing process leads most to abandon deceit and hypocrisy, recognizing the damage they do to basic character and the way they backfire in interpersonal relation-ships. There will always be those who have chosen to continue making wrong choices, to build their lives on deceit. What bet-ter cover than to claim religion as their cloak of righteousness from which to fleece the unwary and gullible? Their very hypocrisy gives the lie to their Christian profession.

The conduct of their daily lives denies the very faith they vociferously embrace. God is not fooled by them. He will per-mit them to exercise their free will for a limited time. Their day in court is coming. They will receive their just reward. Their high public profile places a mighty weapon in Satan's hands. Their public exposure has turned many away from the faith. They have subjected Christianity to ridicule and criticism. Their final judgment will be severe.

The free will aspect of personality is a gift of God. It is not annulled when individuals become Christians. The Christian has become a partaker of God's very own nature with the potential of becoming a Christ-like person in every department of life. Thought patterns and habits of many years' duration are not instantly vaporized upon becoming a Christian. Every person is faced with multiple choices daily. The process of Christian growth in maturity frequently involves painful choices. Choices of self-denial. Choices that put God first and self second. It's always easier to serve self rather than God.

The decision to serve self often gives more immediate gratification. Many Christians choose the easier way. They continue to live lives indistinguishable from the non-Christian masses. Jesus said that we would know the reality of people's lives by their fruits, by what they produce. A merely verbal commitment that leaves a life unchanged is a highly questionable commitment.

A sincere confession of Jesus Christ as Savior and Lord will bring change. God invades the private world of those who have made this choice. He will bring dramatic change over time in one's daily conduct. In one's thought life. In one's treatment of others. In one's financial dealings. Sometimes the process is painfully slow if the individual chooses not to cooperate with God.

Many have been put off by the conduct of professing Christians. They may have said to themselves, "If that person is a Christian, I want nothing to do with Christianity." That approach is tantamount to rejecting the entire concept of free will. Free will permits Christians to make wrong choices. Choices that may be repellent to observers who have moral integrity.

Most honest persons will acknowledge the fact that they do not always live up to their own standards in all the details of their lives, even though they claim no affiliation with any religious group. The offending Christians may have experienced genuine renewal in certain areas of their personal lives. Areas that have not yet been revealed in the external life. Areas of change that are invisible to the outward observer.

There will always be those individuals who claim to have made verbal commitments to the faith merely for the perceived security of an eternal life insurance policy. Few would wish to spend an eternity of potential separation from God if that potential prognosis could be annulled by a simple verbal acknowledgement—inviting Jesus Christ to be one's Savior.

God sees through false motives. He cannot be deceived. The conduct of every individual following the verbal decision will demonstrate its validity. Conduct will prove whether it was genuine or not. The Bible speaks out clearly on this point. "Be not deceived, God is not mocked, for whatsoever a man soweth that shall he also reap. He that soweth to the flesh shall reap corruption, but he that soweth to the Spirit shall of the Spirit reap everlasting life."[4]

APATHY

The physiological response of the common frog may present a powerful illustration of human response to spiritual truth. It is claimed that a frog can be placed in lukewarm water in an open shallow container, leaving it the option of easily jumping out. Then the water can be slowly heated to the boiling point until the frog is cooked to death. It will not jump out to save its life during the slow heating process when it has the opportunity. Why not? Because the extremely slow heating process lulls the frog into a state of extreme apathy toward the potentially lethal heating water. Until it's too late. The very apathy of the frog brought about its own death sentence. The slowly heating water felt good. It didn't seem to be a threat to life. But it brought death. The frog believed a lie. As time unfolded, truth brought death.

In the very same way many individuals adopt a lifestyle that runs counter to God's truth and His spiritual laws. Involvement with immorality. Substance abuse. People abuse. Selfishness. Dishonesty. These things seem to be nearly normal responses to life's circumstances. They often feel good to us. Just like the warming water felt to the frog. They offer an immediate reward. Seemingly! Yet the God-given conscience is slowly and steadily being eroded. Violated. Bludgeoned into insensibility, ever so slowly and imperceptibly.

Initial violations of conscience will be rewarded by guilt. As the behavior is engaged in again and again, the conscience slowly becomes inoperable, as though it never existed. Now nearly anything goes without remorse. Just like the slow heating process. Guilt is a thing of the past. A numbing apathy has taken over.

No thought is given to the unfolding of truth in its future dimension. The inner moral world of the secret thought life has become lulled into a near comatose state spiritually. The sting has succeeded. The future holds a dismal prospect for such individuals. The poison of the sting has immobilized them spiritually. The grace of God alone offers them hope—the penetration of His truth cutting deep through the morass of moral disintegration with convictions that restore the conscience and bring new life. New personal power to resist temptation.

A powerful new realization of truth's unfolding consequences will develop. Consequences resulting in eternal tragedy for every individual who lives for self and rejects truth. If you feel apathetic toward God's truth, beware. Analyze the reasons. Take an honest spiritual inventory.

Are you living for self? Are all your personal goals focused on getting the best for yourself? Are you engaged in immorality? How about in your secret thought life? Doing anything dishonest? What priority does God have in your life? Not just externally, but in your private personal world. If you let the course of your life continue in these patterns, you're going to crash. Just like the frog. The end result is death. Spiritually! You can break free. Get out of the rut. God came to earth only once. So far. He is coming back to set up his earthly kingdom. Future dimensional truth is inexorable, like a slowly moving steam roller. You can't escape it. Get your life on track with truth. Now! Before it's too late. You still have a choice. But for how long? No one knows. We are all simply a heartbeat away from eternity. Beware of apathy.

THE INTELLECTURAL TRAP

The intellect is a major stumbling block. There is a compelling force in the minds of many, often the well educated. A force that motivates the individual to sit in judgment of truth and to maintain a skeptical and highly critical state of mind toward the unmeasurable spiritual realities.

This orientation can serve a valuable function: to steer one away from not so obvious error. It can, however, block such individuals from recognizing real truth when confronted with it. This mind-set has developed the view that often seizes upon every means of discrediting possibilities of truth. Many such individuals of this orientation tend to scoff at faith. Their skepticism has blinded them to the reality of the unmeasurable. They demand measurable physical evidence.

Yet in the very process of rejecting Biblical truth they are embracing faith. A faith whose object is self. A self-faith that is based on one's own intellect—an intellect that has only superficially examined a pseudo-Christianity and rejected it. Most who are of this persuasion have never seriously examined the faith. Their rejection is based on an inaccurate perception. They may have seen individuals who consider themselves Christians, people who in some cases may have been proved charlatans. In other cases they may have seized upon inconsistencies in the lives of certain individual believers, finding them wanting and judging their lives to be sadly lacking in virtue.

It goes without saying that among the scientific community there is a nearly tacit view of the Bible that assumes it to be mere legend. Not worthy of serious study or consideration. Full of contradictions and inconsistencies. This rejection of biblical truth constitutes a faith in self. Although unspoken, an unconscious reliance on one's own intellect begins to develop concurrently with the advance of education.

If you fall into this category, can you demonstrate supernatural qualities in terms of future truth? Have you ever made a long-range prediction that has seen pinpoint fulfillment? Have you made two such predictions? Three? Hundreds? The Bible has. History has proved them true. Have you ever died, been buried, then resurrected? Jesus has! And those few he chose to restore to life.

Do you see how absolutely unique Jesus is in all of human history? No great religious leader in all of human history has ever claimed to be God. Claimed that he would be resurrected!

And subsequently was! But that's the nature of truth. It demands a future dimension. Its future dimension sets it apart from the highest human achievements. And proves it to be supernatural! As the personification of truth in the flesh, Jesus alone in all the epoch of history came to reveal God's truth to the world.

Do you see what an untenable position you are in if you have adopted a self-faith? Even though you may be unaware of having taken that position, you are taking full responsibility for your entire coming eternity. Without the resources to do so. You don't even know what's going to happen to you tomorrow. Even in the next hour. Or minute!

The Bible aptly describes such individuals. Those who have made self the object of their faith. "Stop fooling yourselves. If you count yourself above average in intelligence, as judged by this world's standards, you had better put this all aside and be a fool rather than let it hold you back from the true wisdom from above. For the wisdom of this world is foolishness to God...he (man) stumbles over his own 'wisdom' and falls."[5]

Don't fall into the trap of embracing an intellectual self-faith. It will leave you empty in this life. Bereft of true peace with God. And it will leave you destitute at the grave. Abandoned to your own pitifully inadequate resources.

Jesus describes the response of the truth-rejecting intellectual in his parable of the sower. The intellectual falls into the category of the heart that refuses to give any credibility to the Word of God. You still have a free will. A choice. For a limited time. You can still respond affirmatively to the Word and become the good soil. To produce good things in your life. Things that are eternal in nature. To be a source of continuing blessing to others. Your choice option only remains viable until you die. After that, it's too late. You will be eternally separated from God, according to Jesus Christ. The Man of Truth.

Chapter Six
The Book of Truth

The Bible is comprised of sixty-six individually written books. It includes the writings of forty or more authors. Several authors are responsible for one or more books. The Old Testament segment includes thirty-nine books. It was written during the period from around 1500 B.C. up to 400 B.C. Then came the "silent period" of more than four hundred years before the new Testament was penned. Each Old Testament prophecy regarding the times of Jesus and beyond was written a minimum of four hundred years before its fulfillment. A remarkable demonstration of truth in its future dimension. These dates are very important to remember due to myriad prophecies found in the Old Testament. Prophecies that were fulfilled precisely not only during the Old Testament period, but also in the life of Jesus and beyond.

The New Testament includes twenty-seven books. It was written from around A.D. 40 to around A.D. 90. The word *Bible* is based on the Greek word *Biblos*, a word that translates in English to the word *Testament*. Meaning *covenant* or *agreement*. Perhaps one of the most obvious supernatural elements concerning this series of writings covering a sixteen century period of time is the unity and agreement between all the authors. Without supernatural guidance, how could all these vastly divergent individuals possibly have created all their writings with one coherent theme? In most cases they are separated by hundreds of years of history. Impossible! Humanly impossible in the least. Someone has said, "The Old Testament is the New Testament concealed and the New Testament is the Old Testament revealed." The developing theme of God's plan for mankind beginning in the Old Testament finds its fulfillment in Jesus Christ in the New Testament.

The authors of these Bible books ran the gamut of lifestyles. From kings to farmers. Philosophers to poets. Musicians to princes. Priests to fishermen. From statesmen to tentmakers. Some had formal education. Some had little or none. All were used as God's mouthpieces to communicate His message in the language of the common people, people who lived in each of those historic eras.

God's method is clearly described by the apostle Peter. He states, "Prophecy came not in old time by the will of man: but holy men of God spake as they were moved by the Holy Ghost."[1] These specially chosen men of God recorded God's message of truth as they were moved by His Holy Spirit, communicating God's very own message to His world of created beings. A message of truth! A life-changing message! A message endorsed by its future dimensional truth.

These holy men of God, under the prompting of His Holy Spirit, were directed to place a powerful emphasis on the truth of their message. Here is just a small sampling of the myriad Bible verses on the truth of God as it is recorded in His book of truth:

"He is a God of truth"[2]
"The Lord...abundant in goodness and truth"[3]
"All His works are done in truth"[4]
"...The truth of thy salvation"[5]
"His truth endures to all generations"[6]
"The truth of the Lord endures forever"[7]
"Righteousness and thy law is the truth"[8]
"All thy commandments are truth"[9]
"(God)...which keepeth truth forever"[10]
"The God of truth"[11]

"Jesus saith unto him, I am the way the truth and the life, no man cometh unto the Father but by me"[12]

"I (Jesus) tell you the truth"[13]

"Thy word is truth"[14]

"...Then Jesus answered...to this end was I born, and for this cause came I into the world, that I should bear witness unto the truth. Everyone that is of the truth heareth my voice"[15]

"...The judgment of God is according to truth"[16]

(The Bible is) "The Word of truth"[17]

"The truth of the Gospel"[18]

"He begat us with the word of truth."[20]

Speaking through the prophet Isaiah (circa 750 B.C.), God expresses His relationship to truth in its future dimension. "Everything I prophesied came true, and now I will prophesy again. I will tell you the future before it happens."[21] The nation of Israel was destroyed by the Roman general Titus in A.D. 70. This resulted in the dispersion of the Israelites into many nations of the world. They would build new lives within these foreign cultures, almost without exception gravitating to the upper echelons of their new socio-economic parameters. They would, however, miraculously retain their national identity for nearly two thousand years, until the present era. Their return to their homeland began in the late 1940s when the state of Israel was re-established by United Nations charter.

The following prophecy of Isaiah reaches across two thousand eight hundred years with this remarkable demonstration of future dimensional truth.

> Don't be afraid, for I am with you. I will gather you from east and west, from north and south. I will bring my sons and daughters back to Israel from the farthest corners of the earth. All who claim me as their God will come, for I have made them for my glory. I created them. Bring them back to me blind as they are and deaf when I call (although they see and hear). Gather the nations

together! Which of all their idols ever has foretold such things? Which can predict a single day
ahead? Where are the witnesses of anything they
said? If there are no witnesses, then they must
confess that only God can prophesy.[22]

Here is God's own assertion, speaking through the prophet
Isaiah, asserting the fact that future dimensional truth is impossible for the natural human mind to generate. This pinpoint,
pre-written history demands an acknowledgement of the Bible's
supernatural origin.

Many of us have seen the partial fulfillment of this two thousand eight hundred year old prophecy in our lifetimes through
the restoration of Israel as a nation in 1948 following a two
thousand year period when the Israelites were without a homeland. This launched the world-wide immigration. Many of the
Israelites are returning to the place of their national origin in
our modern-day era.

We must recognize the fact that the God who can and who
has unfurled annals of future human history is the God of truth.
In all its three dimensions. We must see that His truth will
impact every person on the face of the earth. Those who ignore
this supreme creator God of the universe do so at their own
eternal peril.

The creator God of the universe is big enough to have
authored His Word for all mankind. Through human messen-
gers! And guarded its preservation down through the centuries.
To have clear and logical endorsements of it. Believable
endorsements! Endorsements that prove beyond a shadow of a
doubt that it has to be supernatural in origin. You can trust its
God-breathed origin on the basis of its future dimensional
truth! You will soon discover God's life-transforming power if
you so choose, changing your personal world as you commit
your life to Him.

Chapter Seven
The Impact of Future Dimensional Truth

We have already discussed the immutability of truth. Truth that governs the physical laws of the universe in its three dimensions. It seems strange that there are millions of people worldwide who conduct their daily lives as though there are no equally immutable spiritual laws. Laws that govern human relationships. Laws that impact every life no less than the physical laws on our planet.

Perhaps through the process of simple logic we can demonstrate the fact that God has also created spiritual laws—laws that many ignore, but laws that refuse to be vaporized by behavior that contradicts them. The Book of Proverbs (circa 950 B.C.) lists a group of human behaviors. Behaviors described as hated by God.[1] These have occasionally been described as the seven deadly sins.

"For there are six things the Lord hates, no, seven:
(1) haughtiness;
(2) lying;
(3) murdering;
(4) plotting evil;
(5) eagerness to do wrong;
(6) a false witness;
(7) sowing discord among brothers."

(1) HAUGHTINESS OR PRIDE

The primacy of this behavior is very significant. This was the sin that defeated Satan in his initial rebellion against God. He chose to set himself above God rather than to obey and worship Him. In effect, he chose to become his own God. This attitude is the perfect expression of a type person we have all known. They have set themselves above everyone. They must be "always right." They won't listen to anyone. They have all the answers. They consider themselves superior to everyone else. They lack compassion, empathy, and basic human kindness. They are self-centered and manipulative. They have set themselves up as their own god.

They will accept no advice from anyone, much less submit to authority inwardly. They are total-control freaks. They will never acknowledge a wrong. Do we enjoy being with people like that? A history of this type behavior (past truth) has resulted in ruptured relationships, generating misery and loneliness (present truth). Those who sustain this manner of relating will experience the syndrome of rejection—being disliked and shunned.

Our prisons are filled with many such individuals. They have lived for self at the expense of others and have had to be restrained from living in a free society. Their future (future truth) will be predictably bleak and miserable so long as they continue unchanged. God hates pride.

(2) LYING

Who admires a liar? In any culture? All of us have lied at some point in our lives. The list of those who practice lying is a tragic one. Those committing adultery are living a lie. Embezzlers are liars. Political influence peddlers are liars. Thieves are liars. Millions lie on their income tax returns. The entire underground economy is based on lying to the government—lies that are easily justified by shallow excuses.

Advertisers lie about their products. Automobile manufacturers have lied about defects in their cars in spite of multiplied injuries. Tobacco companies have lied to the public for years, resulting in untold tragedy on a world-wide scale. Just to make money. Our courts are choked with lawsuits seeking to redress the unjust consequences of lying.

Extensive lying is often a major player in leading people to a life of crime. Lying begins by lying to one's self. Believing there is greater fulfillment to be found through self-serving dishonesty rather than through hard working integrity. The liar lives in a world of self-delusion. A world that offers no future other than self-destruction. God hates lying!

(3) MURDER

Little need be said about the impact of future truth upon those who violate this spiritual law. The Bible tells us that God created man in His own image. The willful taking of a human life is a direct strike at God. And His highest level of creation. Throughout the Scriptures, God asserts again and again His unconditional love for every individual He has brought into the human race. The murderer kills one greatly loved by God. God alone has reserved the right to decide the time of death. For each person. It is a rebuke to God for anyone to usurp God's plan for a person. There are those who feel they have "gotten away" with a murder. They may have been exonerated by the judicial system. Not so! God has said, "Vengeance is mine, I shall repay, saith the Lord."[2] No murderer has gotten away with his crime. God is patiently waiting the Day of Judgment. The murderer's future is a foregone conclusion apart from the Gospel of God's grace and mercy.

(4) PLOTTING EVIL

The one who plots evil casts aside all honesty, integrity, truthfulness, empathy, and compassion. We have all known of world leaders whose lives have been characterized by plotting evil.

History has cataloged their tragic deeds. Untold millions of innocent human beings have suffered unspeakable horrors at the hands of such men.

Little wonder that this behavior is hated by God. Whether on a nation-wide scale or in the confines of one's private world, every imaginable heinous crime began in the mind and was subsequently pursued through the process of plotting until it was physically acted out. The plotting process can become the vehicle whereby untold evils are hatched. God hates the plotting of evil.

(5) EAGERNESS TO DO WRONG

Eagerness to do wrong involves an attitude. The attitude that rejects the entire concept of a just God who will hold every person accountable on the Day of Judgment. Blatant unbelief in a good creator-God. An attitude that is totally self-serving. Placing one's own desires before all else regardless of the damage done to others.

This principle is responsible for the astronomical crime rate world-wide. Those of this orientation are living under a delusion that riches and selfishness are the key to fulfillment in life. The means of acquiring these self-centered goals seem somehow unimportant. The end justifies the means. The entire concept of accountability to a supreme being somewhere in the future is not even considered. Visualize the transformation in the societies of the world if this behavior were universally rejected. God hates behavior that incorporates eagerness to do wrong.

(6) A FALSE WITNESS

The fact that this is the second behavior on the list that involves lying underscores the intensity of God's hatred for the one who practices it. The motive for lying about what one has witnessed is invariably self-serving. The acceptance of bribes for this behavior is a common motivation.

Another motivation is that of exoneration from incriminating acts or circumstances. Many innocent individuals are wrongfully accused and subsequently punished on the testimony of false witnesses. Truth is distorted to fit the self-serving motives of the liar. God hates behavior culminating in being a false witness.

(7) SOWING DISCORD AMONG BROTHERS

The term brothers suggests a close relationship, one that could involve immediate and extended family members and also the relationship that exists between believers in religious group settings. Self-serving motives involving malicious gossip may be involved here. Jealousy could also be a major player driving the one who creates discord.

Since the Bible declares that God is love, His pattern for family members and church brethren is one of unity and enjoyment of each other. Christ points out the unique nature of Christian love. It is to be an identifiable characteristic. It should set Christians apart as people enjoying a supernatural quality of love for all people. And especially toward fellow Christians. Jesus actually commands us to show love to one another.[3] The individual who either carelessly or purposefully injects conversation that is negative and injurious to others is clearly at cross-purposes with God's design for us. Future truth will reveal loss of respect, deteriorating relationships, distrust, and eventual judgment. God hates behavior that includes the sowing of discord between others.

Basic common sense learned in our culture has long since convinced us that these seven behaviors backfire, resulting in self-destruction for those who insist on using them as a way of life. We have learned this even apart from any religious training. We subconsciously avoid these ways of relating in the world around us. We have discovered that they simply don't work for our good.

If we recognize the reality of God's truth for our present daily lives, why do we find it so hard to believe His truth regarding an eternal relationship with Him? His Word tells us how to live lives of goodness. Integrity. Honor. Deeply rewarding lives. With qualities we all admire. Qualities that develop fulfilled people. And He tells us how to prepare for a far more joyous existence with Him. In eternity. If we see the logic of one, why do we reject the other? The consequences of God's future dimensional truth in our work-a-day world should validate the authenticity of God's truth for our lives in the world to come.

The Bible states unequivocally the mind-bending impact of the choices we make every day in their influence on our future. "For God is closely watching you, and He weighs carefully everything you do. The wicked man is doomed by his own sins; they are ropes that catch and hold him. He shall die, because he will not listen to the truth."[4]

Logically, we can see a cataclysmic collision between God's hatred of these destructive behaviors and His unconditional love for those individuals who practice them. How can such a paradox be reconciled? How could one who practices such conduct possibly be loved by God? How could such a person ever be welcomed into God's eternal kingdom of love, joy, and peace? The startling reality is that, even though all have transgressed these moral boundaries of God, the unconditional love of God offers forgiveness. Freely! And a changed life for all who will believe and receive God's gift of eternal life. God has clearly enunciated His spiritual truth. He will hold every individual on the face of the earth accountable to its standard.

Chapter Eight
Scientific Verification

The purpose of God's Word is to communicate to all mankind His love for the entire human family, including his eternal plan to adopt into His own family all who will believe and receive His gift of eternal life through His son, Jesus Christ. The Bible was not designed to be a science textbook. But since it is the Word of God, and God created the universe, it must be accurate. When it deals with matters relating to science.

Due to the historical chronology of the various individuals who penned the Scriptures, we have a clear picture of the supernatural nature of the Bible when we compare certain scientific observations mentioned in it—observations on scientific facts which were undiscovered until many centuries later by modern science of the times.

Since early antiquity, the sharpest human minds, including men of science, have sought to analyze and explain the physical world. Since some books of the Bible date back three thousand five hundred years, many comparisons are made possible between prevailing scientific views of those eras and Bible references revealing facts that would only be discovered centuries later. These comparisons demonstrate many scientific accuracies in the Bible where science lagged far behind. Consider a few of these instances:

THE HYDROLOGIC CYCLE

The water cycle remained undiscovered by science until the late renaissance period in the early sixteenth century. Some twenty-five hundred years earlier, the writers of Job and Ecclesiastes both described aspects of the water cycle. Job declares: "Behold God is great...For He maketh small the drops of water, they pour down rain according to their vapor which the clouds do drop and distill upon man abundantly."[1]

Ecclesiastes states: "All the rivers run into the sea yet the sea is not full. Unto the place from whence the rivers come thence they return again."[2]

THE CIRCULAR SHAPE OF THE EARTH

The best scientific minds believed the earth to be flat until the sixteenth century. Some fifteen hundred years earlier, the prophet Isaiah stated: It is He who sitteth upon the circle of the earth..." (referring to God).[3] The generally accepted view that the earth was flat was contradicted by Bible truth—truth that advancing science discovered to be true.

SUSPENSION OF THE EARTH IN SPACE

Men of science only discovered that the earth was suspended in space in the early sixteenth century. Some three thousand years earlier, the patriarch Job had declared: "He hangeth the earth upon nothing."[4] Human wisdom took three millennia to catch up with this supernaturally revealed wisdom.

THE ENERGY POWERING THE UNIVERSE IS SLOWLY WEARING DOWN

Two thousand five hundred years before scientists discovered that the energy supplying the universe was wearing down like a wind-up alarm clock, the Psalmist declared: "Of old hast thou laid the foundation of the earth, and the heavens are the work of thy hands. They shall perish, but thou shalt endure, yea all of them shall become old like a garment: Like a vesture shalt thou change them, and they shall be changed."[5] Just as a garment wears out, modern science has discovered that the energy powering the universe is slowly winding down.

BLOOD IS THE SOURCE OF LIFE IN THE HUMAN BODY

By the eighteenth century it became a common medical practice to bleed seriously ill patients. The best medical minds of the times had developed the theory that the sickness could be drained from the body by draining the blood. Modern medical science has recognized the urgency of maintaining the full blood supply. Transfusions are a routine practice for those whose blood supply has been depleted as a result of injuries.

Some historians believe that George Washington's physician, having directed such bleeding, may have inadvertently caused his death. Some three thousand years earlier the Bible declared: "For the life of the flesh is in the blood."[7] Many deaths may have been averted had the eighteenth century physicians heeded this Biblical truth.

MAKEUP OF THE PHYSICAL UNIVERSE

Nineteen hundred years before modern science discovered that the physical world was made up of invisible matter the Bible stated: "The worlds were framed by the Word of God, so that things which are seen were not made of things which do appear."[8]

JET STREAM WINDS

Two thousand six hundred years before modern science discovered the earth's pattern of continuously circulating jet stream winds, Solomon stated: "The wind goeth toward the south, and turneth about unto the north; it whirleth about continually and the wind returneth again according to its circuits."[9]

MAN'S GENETIC MAKEUP

Modern science attained an understanding of genetics in the nineteenth century beginning with the work of Gregor Mendel, published in 1866. Until that era, science had no knowledge regarding the genetic makeup of all life forms. Genes are the blueprint containing all the information which determines the potential development of the mature individual. This information is already present in the DNA molecules of the human spermatozoa and ovum before they are united in the reproductive process.

Nearly three thousand years before these genetic discoveries of modern science, the Psalmist describes this remarkable process. He declares: "Thine eyes did see my substance, yet being unformed, and in thy book all my members were written, which in continuance were fashioned when as yet there was none of them."[10] This verse describes God's role in monitoring the creation of the individual even before the time of conception.

It also points out the fact that all of our members, both physical and mental components, were already determined, describing the genetic blueprint of potential growth and maturity. Included is the fact that this blueprint would be in process ("Which in continuance were fashioned") from the time of conception. It also points out the fact that the code was accurately followed by the subsequent process of growth and maturity.

What a remarkable three thousand year preview of what science would discover three millennia later. The fact that the best of human scientists lagged far behind Biblical assertions on science is ample demonstration of the Bible's supernatural origin. From earliest antiquity, no individual or group has been able to generate this future dimension of truth yet undiscovered. The Bible alone among all documents on the face of the earth can claim this distinction.

Chapter Nine
The Man of Truth

The claims Jesus Christ made regarding himself were startling! Revolutionary! They set him apart in stark contrast with any other great leader in all recorded history. No leader whose life was a force for good has ever demonstrated consistent traits of pride and deception. Had they done so, their character flaws would have soon disqualified them as good and virtuous men. History would soon have discarded them from the annals of those who brought truth and enlightenment to the world.

Who admires a proud and boastful man? These qualities are almost universally seen as serious character flaws. Pride is the basic source of boasting. And it comes at the top of God's most unwanted list for human character. On the contrary, humility is just as universally admired. If Jesus had been boastful, he had many unparalleled opportunities to boast.

He calmed the sea during a storm so fierce that his disciples were terrified for their lives. Without a word of boasting. Before or after! He reversed death, restoring several individuals to life. Surrounded by many witnesses. He healed lepers. The blind. The paralyzed. The immoral. He restored them all to productive and fulfilling lives.

In spite of his many supernatural acts, never once do we find even a suggestion of boasting or self-aggrandizement. Rather, we see a truly humble man. Yet any merely human individual who claimed equality with God would immediately be branded an ego-maniac. A proud and boastful egomaniac. We know that a person of that quality could never have brought such great good to the world. The entire thrust of Jesus' ministry was to reveal truth. The truth that he was the only way to God for all living beings on earth.

We have already presented the fact that pre-written history falls into a supernatural level of achievement it is humanly impossible to generate. Let us examine some pre-written history regarding this God-man who came to earth to reveal truth. Bear in mind the fact that all Old Testament prophecies were given a minimum of four hundred years before the birth of Christ. The following dates used are subject to a few years variance.

PROPHECY 750 B.C.: THE VIRGIN BIRTH (OLD TESTAMENT)

"Therefore the Lord Himself shall give you a sign: Behold the virgin shall conceive and bear a son and shall call his name Immanuel."[1]

A.D. 1: FULFILLMENT (NEW TESTAMENT)

"And in the sixth month the angel, Gabriel, was sent from God unto a city of Galilee, named Nazareth. To a virgin espoused to a man whose name was Joseph, of the house of David; and the virgin's name was Mary. …And the angel said unto her, Fear not Mary; for thou hast found favor with God. And behold, thou shalt conceive in thy womb, and bring forth a son, and shalt call his name JESUS. He shall be great, and shall be called the Son of the Highest; and the Lord God shall give unto him the throne of his father, David. And he shall reign over the house of Jacob forever; and of his kingdom there shall be no end.… And she brought forth her first-born son, and wrapped him in swad-dling clothes, and laid him in a manger, because there was no room for them in the inn."[2]

PROPHECY 750 B.C.: PLACE OF BIRTH
(OLD TESTAMENT)

"But thou, Bethlehem Ephrathah, though thou be little among the thousands of Judah, yet out of thee shall he come forth unto me that is to be ruler in Israel, whose goings forth have been from of old, from everlasting."[3]

A.D. 1: FULFILLMENT (NEW TESTAMENT)

"And Joseph also went up from Galilee,...unto the city of David, which is called Bethlehem...to be registered with Mary, his espoused wife, being great with child.... And she brought forth her first-born son."[4]

PROPHECY EIGHTH CENTURY B.C.:
JESUS IN EGYPT (OLD TESTAMENT)

"...God brought him forth out of Egypt."[5]

A.D. 5: FULFILLMENT (NEW TESTAMENT)

"When he arose, he took the young child and his mother by night, and departed into Egypt: And was there until the death of Herod, that it might be fulfilled which was spoken by the Lord through the prophet, saying, Out of Egypt have I called my son."[6]

PROPHECY 750 B.C.: JESUS WOULD BE PRECEDED
BY A FORERUNNER (OLD TESTAMENT)

"Behold I send my messenger to prepare the way before me, and the Lord whom you seek will suddenly come to His temple; the messenger of the covenant in whom you delight, behold he is coming says the Lord of Hosts."[7]

A.D. 30: FULFILLMENT (NEW TESTAMENT)

"In those days came John the Baptist, preaching in the wilderness of Judea, 'Repent, for the Kingdom of heaven is at hand.' For this is he who was spoken of by the prophet Isaiah when he said, 'The voice of one crying in the wilderness: Prepare the way of the Lord, make his paths straight.'"[8]

PROPHECY 650 B.C.: JESUS' TRIUMPHAL ENTRY (OLD TESTAMENT)

"Rejoice greatly, O daughter of Zion; shout O daughter of Jerusalem; behold, they King cometh unto thee; he is just, and having salvation; lowly, and riding upon an ass and a colt the foal of an ass."[9]

A.D. 32: FULFILLMENT (NEW TESTAMENT)

"And the disciples went, and did as Jesus commanded them, and brought the ass, and the colt, and put on them their clothes, and they set him thereon. And a very great multitude spread their garments in the way; others cut down branches from the trees, and spread them in the way. And the multitudes that went before, and that followed, cried, saying, Hosanna to the Son of David! Blessed is he that cometh in the name of the Lord! Hosanna in the highest!"[10]

PROPHECY 750 B.C.: JESUS' OWN NATION REJECTS HIM (OLD TESTAMENT)

"He is despised and rejected of men, a man of sorrows, and acquainted with grief, and we hid as it were our faces from him; he was despised, and we esteemed him not. Surely he hath borne our griefs, and carried our sorrows; yet we did esteem him stricken, smitten of God, and afflicted. But he was wounded for our transgressions, he was bruised for our iniquities; the chastisement for our peace was upon him, and with his stripes we are healed."[11]

A.D. 32: FULFILLMENT (NEW TESTAMENT)

"When the morning was come, all the chief priests and elders of the people took counsel against Jesus to put him to death; And when they had bound him, they led him away, and delivered him to Pontius Pilate, the governor."[12]

PROPHECY 550 B.C.: JESUS BETRAYED FOR THIRTY PIECES OF SILVER (OLD TESTAMENT)

"And I said unto them., If ye think good, give me my price; and if not, forbear. So they weighed for my price thirty pieces of silver."[13]

A.D. 33: FULFILLMENT (NEW TESTAMENT)

"Then one of the twelve, called Judas Iscariot, went unto the chief priests, And said unto them, What will ye give me, and I will deliver him unto you? And they bargained with him for thirty pieces of silver."[14]

PROPHECY 950 B.C.: JESUS' AGONY ON THE CROSS (OLD TESTAMENT)

"My God, my God, why hast thou forsaken me? …I am poured out like water, and all my bones are out of joint; my heart is like wax; it is melted within me. My strength is dried up like a potsherd, and my tongue cleaveth to my jaws; and thou hast brought me into the dust of death."[15]

A.D. 33: FULFILLMENT (NEW TESTAMENT)

"And about the ninth hour Jesus cried with a loud voice, saying, Eli, Eli, lama sabach thani, that is to say, My God, my God, why hast thou forsaken me? …Jesus when he had cried again with a loud voice, yielded up the spirit."[16]

It should be noted that at the time of the Psalmist's prophecy crucifixion was an uninvented form of torture and death. It was invented by the Romans only a century or so before Christ's crucifixion.

PROPHECY 950 B.C.: JESUS OFFERED VINEGAR ON THE CROSS (OLD TESTAMENT)

"They gave me also gall for my food and in my thirst they gave me vinegar to drink."[17]

A.D. 33: FULFILLMENT (NEW TESTAMENT)

"And when they were come unto a place called Golgotha, that is to say, a place of a skull, they gave him vinegar to drink, mingled with gall; and when he had tasted it, he would not drink."[18]

PROPHECY 950 B.C.: JESUS' HANDS AND FEET WOULD BE PIERCED (OLD TESTAMENT)

"…They pierced my hands and my feet."[19]

A.D. 33: FULFILLMENT (NEW TESTAMENT)

"And it was the third hour; and they crucified him."[20] (Crucifixion involved the piercing of the hands and feet by the nails fastening the victim to the cross.)

PROPHECY 950 B.C.: JESUS' GARMENTS WOULD BE GAMBLED FOR (OLD TESTAMENT)

"They part my garments among them and cast lots upon my vesture."[21]

A.D. 33: FULFILLMENT (NEW TESTAMENT)

"Then the soldiers, when they had crucified Jesus, took his garments, and made four parts, to every soldier a part; and also his coat. Now the coat was without seam, woven from the top throughout. They said, therefore, among themselves, Let us not tear it, but cast lost for it, whose it shall be; that the scripture might be fulfilled, which saith, They parted my raiment among them, and for my vesture they did cast lots. These things, therefore, the soldiers did."[22]

PROPHECY 950 B.C.: JESUS' BONES NOT TO BE BROKEN ON THE CROSS (OLD TESTAMENT)

"Many are the afflictions of the righteous; but the Lord delivereth him out of them all. He keepeth all his bones; not one of them is broken."[23]

A.D. 33: FULFILLMENT (NEW TESTAMENT)

"Then came the soldiers, and broke the legs of the first, and of the other who was crucified with him. But when they came to Jesus, and saw that he was dead already, they broke not his legs."[24]

PROPHECY 950 B.C.: JESUS WOULD BE RAISED FROM THE DEAD (OLD TESTAMENT)

"Therefore my heart is glad, and my glory rejoiceth; my flesh also shall rest in hope. For thou wilt not leave my soul in sheol, neither wilt thou permit thine Holy One to see corruption."[25]

A.D. 33: FULFILLMENT (NEW TESTAMENT)

"Jesus saith unto them, Come and dine. And none of the disciples dared ask him, Who art thou? knowing that it was the Lord. This is now the third time that Jesus showed himself to his disciples, after he was risen from the dead."[26]

THE CLAIMS OF JESUS CHRIST

We have established the fact that Jesus was neither proud nor boastful. On the contrary. He was marked by great humility. How then can we account for the supernatural claims he made for himself? Claims never before having been heard by any great religious leader. If Jesus was merely human these claims would have been the essence of pride and boastfulness. The startling fact about his claims is a stark contrast with all other great world religions. Jesus' claims revolve around a relationship to himself, never to any system of external works as all other world religions require for their adherents. Observe closely some of his claims.

JESUS: THE EXCLUSIVE AVENUE TO GOD

He said: "I am the way, the truth, and the life, no man cometh to the Father but by me."[27]

Jesus placed a tremendous emphasis on truth in his discourses. He wanted all to know that his message was reality. Concrete reality. He frequently used the phrase "verily, verily," meaning *truthfully, truthfully,* in order to double the effect of his statements. He used the words *truth* or *truthfully, truthfully* ninety-seven times in his discourses to underline the reality of his message.

JESUS: CO-EQUAL WITH GOD

Jesus stated: "I and my Father are one."[28] His statement was so clearly understood as blasphemy that the following verse asserts: "The Jews took up stones again to stone him." In following verses, when Jesus asked for which of his good works they were stoning him, they replied: "For a good work we stone thee not, but for blasphemy, and because that thou being a man, makest thyself God." What a startling contrast! No other great world religious leader ever claimed to be God! Only Jesus Christ!

JESUS: THE RESURRECTION AND THE LIFE

Jesus claimed to be the resurrection and the life. He stated: "I am the resurrection and the life, he that believeth in me, though he were dead, yet shall he live, and whosoever liveth and believeth in me shall never die."[29] Jesus claims that he is the gateway to an eternal afterlife. For all who will believe in him. What an incredible promise! It boggles the human mind. Never to die? Yes! Never to die! You say, "That's ridiculous; everyone dies." The graveyards give mute testimony to that fact. Our hang-up here is our earthly view. The belief that life as we know it requires the physical body and its functions.

The unmeasurable aspects of soul and spirit are the actual source of our emotional hardware. Hardware that makes life what it is as we know it. The unconscious individual is dead from his or her standpoint. There is no connection with life as one has in a state of consciousness. The body may be alive but the soul and the spirit are in a non-functional mode. They are the actual source of all mental and emotional activity.

Jesus' promise to those who choose to trust him with a life commitment is simple. At the instant of physical death, the mental and emotional experience of life will continue. Uninterrupted! In the same mode that was experienced before physical death. But in an unspeakably heightened sense of joyousness. And inexpressible delight.

The apostle Paul underscores this truth of uninterrupted life. After physical death occurs. He states: "We are confident I say, and willing rather to be absent from the body and to be present with the Lord."[30] The experience of the Christian when the body dies is to be instantly translated into the presence of the Lord. What a preposterous claim it would be for any merely human individual to make, no matter how great his worldly achievements. To claim the power to translate those who died physically into the presence of God—any person who made such a claim today would be in big trouble. He or she would likely be placed in a psychiatric facility for observation. In spite of these obvious facts, there are many well-educated, thoughtful people the world over who accept Jesus as a great man but reject his claims of divinity.

How could he have been a great man if his claims of equality with God were lies and deception? Obvious untruths. These claims were the heart and soul of his message. His very claim to be God brought about his death on the cross. The Gospel of Matthew states: "And the high priest answered and said unto him, 'I adjure thee by the living God, that thou tell us whether thou be the Christ, the son of God.' So Jesus saith unto him, 'Thou hast said, nevertheless, I say unto you, hereafter shall ye see the Son of man sitting on the right hand of power, and coming in the clouds of heaven.' Then the high priest tore his clothes, saying, 'He hath spoken blasphemy...they answered and said 'he is guilty of death.'"[31]

JESUS: HIS PURPOSE IN COMING TO EARTH

In Jesus' conversation with Pontius Pilate, the apostle John relates: "Pilate therefore said unto Him, Art thou a King then? Jesus answered: Thou sayest that I am a King. To this end was I born and for this cause came I into the world, that I should bear witness unto the truth. Everyone that is of the truth heareth my voice." Here, Jesus summarized his entire purpose in coming to earth: to reveal to all mankind the realities of truth and its future impact on all living beings. Truth will inexorably unfold. Nothing can stop it. It will not yield to accommodate those who fail to embrace it. The Book of Truth revealed the coming to earth of Jesus more than a thousand years before his arrival. His coming proved the veracity of the Bible and the very obvious fact that the Bible is of supernatural origin, God's message to all mankind.

JESUS: SOURCE OF JOY AND PEACE

Distress, depression, worry, anxiety, fear, confusion, rage, resentment, and many other unwelcome emotions are frequent daily experiences for many the world over. Jesus recognized these common stresses that rob people of a peaceful life. The emotional assault of and consequent preoccupation with frustrating people and circumstances are an ongoing reality in the lives of untold millions the world over. Jesus said: "These things I have spoken unto you, that in me ye might have peace. In the world ye shall have tribulation, but be of good cheer; I have overcome the world." Our trials need no longer rob us of an underlying experience of peace in our daily lives. We can enjoy his peace.

Jesus also stated: "Ask and ye shall receive, that your joy may be full." Life can be a humdrum existence. Of sometimes quiet desperation! There may be occasional times of fun and superficial thrills, but no foundational joy, penetrating the fabric of daily existence. Jesus is the source of our personal power. Power linking us to God. Bringing the reality of God's presence into our private worlds. Jesus clearly proclaims that we all have the potential for joyous daily living. A quality of joy that will penetrate even the most frustrating circumstances.

This experience of joy-infusing friendship with God is waiting for all who will place their trust in Jesus Christ. What logical, clear-thinking man or woman on the face of the earth could possibly reject these indescribable gifts? Gifts that God freely bequeaths. Upon all those who respond to His invitation personally to know Him through His Son, Jesus Christ.

JESUS: TO BE RESURRECTED FROM THE DEAD

Jesus foretold the fact that he would be personally and bodily raised from the dead. This may be one of the most difficult of all Christian doctrines for the non-Christian individual to accept. Nearly everyone has seen death and been exposed to it. We have all seen death to be the great equalizer. No one escapes! Rich. Poor. The brilliant. The average. The mentally handicapped. The sick. The healthy. The celebrity. The leaders. The followers. All will die! Never to be seen again on this earth in living form.

There is one man in history who not only reversed the death process for himself, but even predicted while he was still living that he would do exactly that. In order to certify the fulfillment of his seemingly preposterous prediction, he made seventeen live appearances! Following his death and burial! Seventeen! He made his appearances not to one or two, but to more than five hundred people!

The apostle Paul, describing Jesus' resurrection, makes this statement: "For I delivered unto you first of all that which I also received, that Christ died for our sins according to the Scriptures. And that he was seen of Cephas, then of the twelve.

After that he was seen of above five hundred brethren at once of whom the greater part remain unto this present time, but some are fallen asleep. After that he was seen of me also, as of one born out of due time."[35]

So vast and so diverse a group of witnesses could not possibly have implemented so great a conspiracy. Paul's implication, when he makes the statement that "Many who saw Jesus after his death are themselves still alive," is, in effect: If you don't believe me, you have hundreds still living. Go and verify Jesus' resurrection by talking to them first hand. They will verify the fact for you that Jesus reversed his death appearing to hundreds after the fact. What an earth-shaking truth!

Could Jesus be other than God? And have complete power over death? No human being who ever lived in all the history of mankind ever made this claim. That he would be raised from the dead! Jesus alone made that claim! Then he did exactly as he predicted! What a conclusive demonstration that he was God in the flesh!

The Gospel of Mark states: "And he began to teach them that the Son of man must suffer many things, and be rejected by the elders, and by the chief priests, and scribes, and be killed, and after three days rise again."

On another occasion, contending with the religious leaders, he proclaimed: "Destroy this temple and in three days I will raise it up. Then said the Jews, Forty and six years was this temple in building, and wilt thou raise it up in three days? But he spoke of the temple of his body. When therefore he was raised from the dead, his disciples remembered that he had said this unto them; and they believed the Scripture, and the word which Jesus had said."[37]

Observe the uniqueness of Jesus' claims. They all contrast greatly with every other world religion. All other religions have certain religious duties to perform. The fulfillment of these duties is said to put the adherent "right with God." The basis of these religious observances is essentially a legal relationship. The contrast with Christianity focuses precisely here. Jesus' claims all relate to placing faith in a person. His person. Thus the basis of Christianity is a relationship with the person of Jesus Christ. It is relational in nature. Not legalistic. Not based on performance goals. But an inner re-creating that results in a new set of values. Values that change the outward behavior from the inside. The apostle Paul states: "If any one is in Christ, he is a new creation; the old has passed away, behold the new has come."[38]

The basic problem with belief systems that have legalistic tasks to perform is this: It is quite possible to meet every one of these external standards and leave the heart entirely unchanged. Jesus tells us that our hearts need to be re-created. External observances will never solve our heart problem. The danger in these systems is here: they lull the adherent into a false sense of security. Those who fall into these legalistic patterns play right into the hands of Satan's cosmic sting operation. A careful and honest examination of the inner personal world of our thought lives will immediately expose our need. For a new heart.

JESUS, THE MESSIAH: LONG PROMISED SAVIOR OF ISRAEL

In the Gospel of John, a conversation between Jesus and a Samaritan woman reveals this wonderful truth for Israel! "The woman saith unto him, I know that Messiah cometh, which is called Christ: when he is come he will tell us all things. Jesus saith unto her, I that speak unto thee am he."[39]

Remarkable! What an arrogant and insane claim this would be for a merely human individual to make. An untenable contradiction if Jesus was a great man! Only!

Chapter Ten

Becoming a Christian

The decision to trust God's Word implicitly, to commit one's entire personal world and one's future to Jesus Christ, clear into eternity, is a choice fraught with uncertainty and fear for many. So many doubts assail the mind. What if it doesn't work? Why are there so many other religions with good people? What about the heathen who have never heard?

Satan, God's enemy and the enemy of every living soul, has much at stake in this issue.

His goal is to deceive. Sidetrack. Undermine. And control the spiritual life of every person on earth. He knows full well that the individual who sincerely makes this choice will be forever beyond his reach. He will, therefore, present every possible negative thought to the interested inquirer. To get him or her to reject choosing Christ as Savior.

These kinds of thoughts may also clamor to be heard in one's self-talk: "My friends and family will think I'm a fanatic." "My peers at work will laugh and think I'm a simpleton." "Christianity is really only a crutch for weak people. Mature people don't need it." "If it is true, why do I know so many professing Christians who are phonies?" "This is just too easy. There's no such thing as a free lunch." "You can't take religion too seriously." "Science has long since disproved the Bible. It's just a bunch of myths." "It would really upset my parents. They don't believe this stuff." "I don't have enough money in my budget to pay tithes to some church." "My girlfriend/boyfriend would be upset. They may want to dump me." "I have too much fun going places and doing things on Sundays. I don't want to ruin them by having to go to church every week." "Who could really believe all those ridiculous miracles in the Bible? Besides, it's full of contradictions." "I've lived a good life by society's standards. And all good people go to heaven."

The "prince of the power of the air" has been eminently successful with his unique ability to transmit these kinds of thoughts. To your inner personal world and mine. This mode of his cosmic sting operation has persevered down through the history of mankind from generation to generation. He is committed to the destruction of our souls. Yours and mine! And everyone. That's his goal. He has the power. He has the resources. Look at the indescribable evil he has perpetrated in the world. Pick up any newspaper. Listen to any newscast. You will quickly discover what a major player he has become. Everywhere. All the time.

That's why our strongest weapon against him is truth. That's why God has chosen to reveal truth to us. By giving us pre-written history. Telling us of the coming of His Son to earth. We know that is humanly impossible. Only God can do that. Precise. Specific. Complete prophecies. Made hundreds and hundreds of years before his arrival on earth. How strange that with such supernatural methodology, men and women should find it so difficult to believe. To trust. To commit their lives to such a loving heavenly Father.

One of the most difficult things about making the decision to become a Christian is this: the seeming triviality. The insignificance of the act itself. Many say: "I'd like to believe, and to receive Christ as my Savior. But I simply can't." It is much more a matter of won't than can't. The Bible tells us that nothing in this universe was created apart from Jesus Christ.[1] As our creator, he designed our spiritual dimensions. With a capacity to know and enjoy him. His invitation to become a part of his eternal family lies within the reach of every individual on earth.

Jesus addresses the will. He asks us to make a decision. To exercise our will. To follow him. In sincerity.

Consider thoughtfully these invitations of Jesus:

"For God loved the world so much that he gave his only son so that anyone who believes in him shall not perish but have eternal life."[2]

"...whoever drinks of the water that I shall give him will never thirst; the water that I shall give him will become in him a spring of water welling up to eternal life."[3]

"Truly, truly, I say to you, he who hears my word and believes him who sent me, has eternal life; he does not come into judgment, but has passed from death to life."[4]

"I am the living bread which came down from heaven; if any one eats of this bread, he will live forever..."[5]

"Again Jesus spoke to them, saying, 'I am the light of the world; he who follows me will not walk in darkness, but will have the light of ife.'"[7]

"I am the door; if any one enters by me, he will be saved."[7]

"Jesus said to her, 'I am the resurrection and the life; he who believes in me, though he die, yet shall he live, and whoever lives and believes in me shall never die...'"[8]

"...I am the way, and the truth, and the life; no one comes to the Father, but by me."[9]

"Hitherto you have asked nothing in my name; ask, and you will receive that your joy may be full."[10]

"I have said this to you, that in me you may have peace. In the world you have tribulation; but be of good cheer, I have overcome the world."[11]

"And this is eternal life, that they know thee the only true God, and Jesus Christ whom thou hast sent."[12]

"Pilate said to him, 'So you are a king?' Jesus answered, 'You say that I am a king. For this I was born, and for this I have come into the world, to bear witness to the truth. Every one who is of the truth hears my voice.'"[13]

These invitations of Jesus don't mince words. They are clear. Their appeal is to the will. Any person on earth can choose to respond. Jesus unabashedly presents himself as Almighty God come to earth to reveal God's truth to all mankind. All historical Bible prophecies saw pinpoint accuracy. We have examined only a few. They became the present realities of their time. As they were fulfilled. Jesus' pronouncements regarding each person's future will be no different.

After having considered the evidence supporting the claims of Jesus, the seemingly trivial act of choosing to personalize his message is not difficult. We suggested earlier that all of us live in a personal world of unmeasurable emotional-spiritual dimensions. Dimensions that won't succumb to the test tube. The volitional decision to invite Jesus to invade and rule over that world is included in those dimensions. It is quite natural for us to feel that the unmeasurable is non-existent.

We have lived our lives in an entirely physical world for many years. We have often failed to recognize the unmeasurable aspects of our personhood. Yet these dimensions make up the realities of our daily lives. These kinds of thoughts assail our minds. "Since God is invisible and unmeasurable, how can He actually exist?" "Is He really real?" "Is this decision to follow Jesus just another self-delusional mind game?" "Am I kidding myself simply because I want an insurance policy for my afterlife?" "An afterlife that just might possibly exist?" "Am I doing this just in case?"

Have you ever felt jealousy? Resentment? Ever experienced compassion? Fear? Anger? Hatred? Joy? Certainly you have! As have all normal human beings. All of these dimensions which exist in our private worlds and many more are vital, powerful forces. They are also physically unmeasurable. We, as the disciple

Thomas, somehow feel that we must have physical evidence before we are willing to make a commitment of faith. God is just as real as these powerful forces that formulate our daily lives. The emotions that make up the substance of who we are.

Don't permit the enemy of your soul to trivialize this life-changing decision to place your faith in Jesus Christ. To join his potentially joyous community of followers—souls that are ticketed for an ever deepening, creative, intertwining relationship with their Creator. A secure and joyful relationship. One that will reach into the innermost depths of your personal world. And right on into eternity!

This seemingly trivial choice is the most significant life-impacting decision which you will ever be faced with. No one can begin a relationship with God without first acknowledging personal responsibility. Responsibility for the wrong choices we all have made. We have all transgressed sexually. If not in deed, then in our thought lives. We have all lied. We have all hurt others. Through selfish, unkind, critical attitudes and statements. We have all come under God's judgment as a result. The judgment of condemnation. The Bible says that "All have sinned and come short of the glory of God."[14] Jesus stated unequivocally that all those who had not committed to him were condemned already.[15]

These clear declarations make it eminently clear that sin had a devastating effect on everyone. It is universal and it results in eternal condemnation. The individuals on death row have been condemned by a human court. They are awaiting an execution date. Similarly, those who have not responded to Jesus' invitation are also on death row, awaiting their time of physical death. To be cast out of God's presence. Forever!

The criminal is imprisoned by physical restraint. The unbeliever is in the bondage of spiritual restraint. Bondage to many things. Self-centeredness. Lust. Dishonesty. Unbreakable habits. The list goes on. Some of us tend to feel that we have kept the Ten Commandments. And are therefore ticketed for heaven. Satan has deceived us. Our sociological comparison factors have exonerated us in our own eyes. We discussed this earlier. Most middle-class citizens operate with a modicum of basic honesty. At least outwardly. We are not involved in violent acts of lawlessness. We are considered to be "good" people by our friends and by our society in general.

God's Ten Commandments paint a drastically different picture. Let's see how we measure up to God's standard in the light of them.

The First Commandment states: "You shall have no other gods before me." We tend to interpret this as gods other than the God of the Bible, such as those of other religions. Idols perhaps. Essentially what we refer to as heathen gods. We're okay on this Commandment, we think. But wait a minute. Let's take a closer look. The concept God is communicating there refers to the issue of giving Him absolute and primary prominence in our entire lives. That includes our inner personal thought life. It also includes our motives. The thoughts we choose to think. And the things we do. Self-centered desires. And our daily decisions. The self-serving ones. That ignore the needs of others.

The major issue is that we make ourselves our own God by our selfishness. And this behavior keeps God at arm's length. What are your inner thoughts engaged with mostly? During the times you're not directly engaged with a physical or mental task that demands your full attention? God, as the creator of our mental, emotional, and physical makeup, knows precisely what the focus of our innermost thinking is. That's how He is able to zero in on us so precisely with these Commandments. Although our thought patterns are occupied with a variety of subjects, they all tend to follow a common thread. A thread basic to the vast majority of them. Selfishness! Always wanting the best for ourselves.

This basic motive launched the entire concept of sin initially! Satan chose to break free from submission to God. He wanted more power. More authority. More status. He wanted to be his own god! Every person on earth has chosen the same path ever since. At least in their early lives. Prior to maturity, we all want to do our own thing. And many continue with this pattern. All their lives. This response is based on our refusal to submit to the authority of our Creator. Over our everyday lives. Our inner private worlds. We seem subconsciously afraid that if we submit to him, God will wring every last bit of fun out of our lives.

The Second Commandment directs us not to make idols for ourselves and not to worship or serve them. A number of religions revere idols or statues of one type or another. Most of the Western world is not involved in this kind of idol worship. The idol of the Western world is materialism. Preoccupation with things money can buy. The status that goes with wealth or fame. Automobiles. Boats. Fine homes. Lavish vacations. Expensive clothing. Sporting events. Trophy-type girlfriends or wives. Celebrity status. An inner personal world given over to frequent fantasies. Fantasies of lust. Wealth. Material acquisitions. Few of us are free of these thoughts. We encourage them and allow them to play through our minds. Over and over. If we are to be honest in our self-appraisal, we must all acknowledge that we have broken this commandment. We have allowed our fantasies to supplant God's rightful place in our private personal worlds.

The Third Commandment forbids taking God's name in vain. One of the more frequent expressions heard today is "Oh my God." This expression is used in situation after situation. Times that have nothing whatever to do with prayer or reverence for God. There is no recognition of God's holiness. It's simply another expression used without God in mind. The use of God's name in profanity is so common that many who use it haven't a clue that they are violating a Commandment of God's. Few are guiltless of disobeying this Commandment.

The Fourth Commandment tells us to "Remember the Sabbath day to keep it holy." God required an entire day in the Old Testament in which He was to be the focus of every thought and activity. The secular world in general has completely bypassed the entire concept of a day dedicated to God. All the days of the week seem to have merged into the same process of daily activities. Little thought is given to concentration on God on any certain day. For the Christian, every day becomes a day of fellowship with God.

The Fifth Commandment enjoins us to honor our father and mother. Most of us, especially during our teenage years, violated this principle. In many cases we sustained an ongoing conflict with our parents, rejecting their advice and counsel. Sometimes blatantly disobeying them. At least in our thought lives. Seeking only self-centered realization of our own goals. Many have manipulated their parents, using them and their resources with little consideration as to how these schemes would negatively impact them.

Thousands of aging and helpless parents across the country are "throwaways" rarely or if ever even visited or encouraged by their selfish children—children who were nourished, loved, and cared for from infancy through adulthood by these very same parents.

The Sixth Commandment tells us not to commit murder. The vast majority of us tend to feel this is one Commandment we have not transgressed. The apostle John sheds additional light on the murderer. He tells us that everyone who hates someone is a murderer.[17] Ever hated anyone? This is another area where most of us have transgressed. Jesus even stated that simply giving another an abusive tongue-lashing puts us in the category of a murderer.[18] This "shoe" fits us all.

The Seventh Commandment forbids committing adultery. This seems reassuring to those of us who have not done that. Jesus reinterprets this Commandment. He tells us that to look lustfully at a member of the opposite sex is the equivalent of committing adultery with them.[19] It's highly likely that no normal male is guiltless on this count. Many females may likely fall into this category as well with the situation reversed. Many allow sexual fantasies to parade through their secret thought lives. Frequently! This Commandment is additional proof demonstrating how far short we fall in meeting God's standard of personal holiness.

The Eighth Commandment forbids stealing. Certainly all have taken something which did not belong to them at some point in their lives. Employee theft from business and industry has grown dramatically in recent years. Insurance scams are a frequent national indiscretion. Economists estimate that the United States has an underground economy in the neighborhood of two hundred million dollars annually. Myriad transactions are made daily without declaring the taxes required. Employers pay employees "under the table" in order to avoid the higher cost of doing business honestly. It's easy to get away with this kind of dishonesty. But God sees us. In all we do. And think. Will God require accountability from us in such small details? Absolutely! Keeping money owed to the government is stealing, no matter how we may try to justify it.

Political influence peddling is another form of theft. The politician offers influence for personal gain. Personal gain that is withheld from the public. Therefore dishonest. Ever been given too much change by a store clerk? Did you return it? If not, that was stealing too. Oops! Another Commandment we've broken!

The Ninth Commandment forbids lying. It's doubtful that any honest adult would claim never to have told a lie. It seems so natural for some. Many have developed this technique into the fine art of making lying a part of everyday life. Justifying themselves in their own eyes. We all stand guilty as charged when it comes to lying.

The Tenth Commandment forbids covetousness. This simply says that we are not to desire anything that is not presently ours. To knowingly encourage fantasies. Of wealth. Sex. Status. Material possessions. Longing for anything that appeals to us. These thoughts qualify as covetousness. There is not a living person on the earth who has not violated this principle. This is no doubt one of the easiest commandments of all to violate. It can go on in our heads day after day, year after year, undetected by those around us. It lies within the realms of our invisible inner personal world. A world that only God can monitor. And does. He knows exactly what we are thinking.

Here is a scary thought. The Bible declares that covetousness is idolatry.[20] That means we are all idolaters. How so? We don't worship little idols! The person who is engaged with a fantasy life revolving around things wanted is displacing God. From the thought life. And replacing Him with self! Self becomes our idol!

An honest reality check of our inner thought life will quickly reveal that we have all broken God's Commandments. If not all, certainly most of them. Can any living person on earth meet this impossible standard? Not one! And this was God's whole purpose. He erected a standard of holiness that could produce only despair in everyone who honestly seeks holiness. All who have honestly tried to keep the Commandments have quickly come face-to-face with the impossibility of doing so. It is therefore impossible to be justified before God on the basis of His Commandments.

The apostle Paul expressed this dilemma. He stated: "When I want to do good, I don't; and when I try not to do wrong, I do it anyway. Now if I am doing what I don't want to, it is plain where the trouble is: Sin still has me in its evil grasp. It seems to be a fact of life that when I want to do what is right, I inevitably do what is wrong."[21]

Even a religious zealot like the apostle Paul, who devoted his entire life to keeping God's law, had to acknowledge honestly his failure to find exoneration through his efforts.

There is an impassable gulf separating God and His holiness from man and his sinfulness. We could describe it as the cosmic sin barrier. It utterly excludes all from approaching God on the basis of self-effort. But here comes the incredible news! "For God was in Christ, restoring the world to himself, no longer counting men's sins against them but blotting them out. This is the wonderful message he has given us to tell others. We are Christ's ambassadors. God is using us to speak to you: We beg you, as though Christ himself were here pleading with you, receive the love he offers you—be reconciled to God. For God took the sinless Christ and poured into him our sins. Then, in exchange, he poured God's goodness into us!"[22]

In other words, Christ willingly paid the penalty for our sins. And God accepted this payment for every man, woman, and child on this earth who by simple faith in his atonement will embrace him as their personal Lord and Savior. Allowing him to transform their inner personal world. Granting him the deciding voice in their every decision. This is the entire meaning and purpose of life. The joyous, fulfilling, potential quality of life for which God created us.

The first step in receiving this wonderful gift of eternal life is this: a personal acknowledgement! Our admission of the unwelcome truth that we have made wrong choices. These choices have violated God's laws. The Bible calls this sin. Each of us is personally responsible for our own transgressions. They have cut us off from God. But God will hold us personally accountable for them if we reject Christ's death on our behalf!

We are all in a desperate dilemma. Cut off from God! Eternally! Living under the sentence of eternal condemnation. Living in daily bondage to selfishness and the many debilitating habits that result from it. God alone had the resources to end the alienation of mankind from Himself. As a just and perfectly holy God somehow sin had to be blotted out. Justified. Atoned for. How to brink this impassable gulf? How to remove this cosmic sin barrier? Since man was unable to justify himself, God would have to do it for him. This is the dilemma that precipitated God's salvation plan.

He would come to earth! In a human body. Become a man. So God entered the mainstream of human history. Born of a woman. Fully human. But fully God! Born just like every other human who had ever been born. Throughout human history. Only without a human father.[23] This had to be in order to break the chain of inheritance that contained the fallen nature. A nature that would inevitably become involved with sin. Think of it: Is there a human being who has ever lived who never sinned? Except Jesus Christ? No!

God Himself, through His Holy Spirit, fathered this child. It all happened two thousand years ago. It had all been prophesied. Hundreds and hundreds of years before his birth. Approximately three hundred prophecies. In the Old Testament. Scriptures written from around 1500 B.C. up to 400 B.C. Future dimensional truth. Supernatural truth.

Jesus lived a sinless and holy life. A life of loving. Healing. Giving himself to every need he saw. But God mysteriously somehow allowed all the evil forces of organized religion to kill him on a cross. Incorporating all the cruelty, brutality, and torture the Roman empire had come up with as punishment for the most heinous criminals. But he didn't deserve it. He was righteous. Holy. Blameless. He had healed the sick. The lame. The blind. Lepers. The immoral.

God's justice was satisfied. His Son's unjust death was sufficient for all the sins of mankind. For every individual on earth. Past. Present. And future! Now God's gift of eternal life could be freely offered. To every living soul on earth.

The qualifications for receiving this gift of eternal life? A Ph.D.? A bachelor's degree? A high school diploma? Giving great sums of money to charity? Dedicating your life to the poor and suffering? Earning a seminary degree? Being a priest? Pastor? Church leader? Church membership? Membership in a secret order? Membership in a country club? Teaching Sunday school? Having lived a good, crime-free life? Doing good deeds? Reading the Bible? Never!

There is nothing we can do to qualify! Forget it! Only by simple faith. Believing that Jesus Christ is God's Son. And that he paid our personal sin penalty. On the cross. His act of self-sacrifice put us right with God by agreeing with God that our wrong choices have cut us off from Him. By being willing to let Him turn our lives around. Recreating us into His own image. Becoming loving, giving people. Receiving the new nature that comes with the gift of His Holy Spirit as the result of our simple faith.

THE BIBLICAL MEANING OF THE TERM *FAITH*

Since the only way God will receive us is by faith, what is faith actually? The English word faith may seem to have a superficial meaning to many. It is an abstract term. It can leave many in a state of uncertainty. Even frustration. Since it is an abstraction, it may seem a precarious first rung on the ladder leading to God. If God is real, why doesn't He simply show Himself to all the world's population? In all of His awesome power and presence? Then everyone on earth could easily believe in Him.

Why does He require us to exercise faith in an invisible cosmic personage? This opens the door to so much doubt and uncertainty. Faith by its very nature seems to open one up to the concept of self-delusion. Since it's an invisible abstraction, am I only kidding myself into believing something I want to believe? Everybody wants to go to heaven. Are we building a self-delusional abstraction into a pacifying concept in order to assuage our uncertainty about the afterlife?

We tend to think that if only God would show Himself physically to all the world, then all would embrace Him. History contradicts this view. God did show Himself physically. To a centralized nation of what was then the known world. Israel. In the person of Jesus Christ. The myriad miracles he performed demonstrated conclusively that he was God come to earth. Drastically unlike any other human being who had ever lived. In all human history.

Resurrecting a number of individuals from the dead. Including himself. Restoring righteous living to prostitutes and thieves. Calming a raging storm at sea with just a few words. Restoring demoniacs to sanity. Supplying thousands with food from a few fishes and loaves of bread. Supplying or positioning vast numbers of fish. For fishermen who had worked all night. Unsuccessfully. Professionals. Who knew what they were doing.

Jesus proved by these and many other supernatural acts that he was precisely who he said he was. God in the flesh. What was the response of the Israelites to a man who had done nothing but good? Supernatural good. Everywhere he went. They crucified him! He became too great a threat to the religious fundamentalists of his day. They had to dispose of him to preserve the status-quo. So much for the idea of God presenting Himself to earth physically. He has done it already. And he was rejected and killed.

Faith, as the basis of a relationship with God, is a unique and wonderful thing. Every man, woman, and child can qualify. No one has to perform religious traditions at any level. The Bible describes faith as a fundamental necessity in order to approach God. Without faith, it is impossible to please Him. The Bible declares: "Now faith is the substance of things hoped for, the evidence of things not seen."[24]

The afterlife is described in the Bible as eternal life. Eternal life is supernatural in nature. It is a quality of life that can only be experienced as we allow Christ to live through us by faith. The old self-serving responses are exchanged for supernatural responses. By faith. Giving. Loving. Serving responses. Responses that result in self-denial. Giving rather than receiving. Self-effort no longer avails. Faith is the connection that brings the power of Jesus Christ into the shoe leather of our moment-by-moment circumstances.

Faith is the substantial reality of having Christ dwelling within the unmeasurable spectrum of our inner private world. The remarkable truth is that this quality of eternal life can begin—and should begin—immediately following our commitment to Christ as our Savior and Lord as we exercise our faith. And to the extent that we exercise our faith.

THE BIBLICAL MEANING OF THE TERM *BELIEVE*

Someone has said that modern-day Christianity in the Western world is presently in a day of "Easy Believism." Many have given a superficial verbal consent to "accepting Christ"— some 60 percent in the U.S. according to polls. Somehow a great number of these individuals have failed to demonstrate their faith. By changed lives. Family violence, Crime, Drug abuse, Immorality, Alcoholism, and basic individual honesty speak volumes. Volumes that give unwavering contradiction to those statistics.

Alleged converts to Christ whose lives continue without demonstrable change are without Biblical precedent. A genuine conversion experience will make itself known early on in the individual's life. First to the convert himself. Next to his or her family. Subsequently in every personal relationship sustained by that person.

We have already suggested that nearly every thoughtful person would certainly wish for heaven as an eternal state. Even though they may be uncertain of the existence of heaven or hell, they may feel that just in case these places do actually exist, why not verbalize the appropriate words? Words that are designed to qualify them for heaven. Meanwhile, hoping their confession involves as little as possible inconvenience to their present lifestyle. These types of conversions may be little more than humanistic effort. God knows the human heart. He made it. He knows the level of sincerity involved.

One of the problems with these shallow confessions may be in the contrast of meaning between the English meaning of the term *believe* and the meaning of the same term in the original Greek of the first century, the language from which our New Testament was translated. Our modern definition of the term *believe* frequently carries a superficial meaning. For example, a person is asked whether he or she thinks it's going to rain. The reply might be, "I believe so." Or perhaps, "Believe me, it will." The inquirer doesn't take these answers with any certainty of fulfillment.

One may ask a friend who he or she thinks will win a certain sporting event. The answer will only be pure conjecture. The answer may sound positive. "I believe the Forty Niners will win." Somehow the word believe has fallen on hard times. It is taken very lightly by many.

Various pollsters have reported that around ninety percent of Americans claim to "believe in God." In light of the proliferating crime statistics, that belief seems to have left our nation entirely unaffected. Levels of morality and integrity continue to erode at an alarming pace. What's wrong? Why this seeming contradiction? The fact is the original language contains an entire package. A package that our English fails to communicate.

In the original language, to believe in the Lord Jesus Christ includes:

To adhere to Jesus;
To trust in Jesus;
To cling to Jesus;
To rely on Jesus;
To give one's self up to Jesus;
To take self out of one's own keeping and to let Jesus keep us.

Observe the dramatic contrast! Between our superficial view of believe and that of the Biblical language. Our view: a mere shallow mental assent. At best an intellectual acknowledgement. An acknowledgement that can leave the conduct of one's inner personal world entirely unchanged. In contrast with the true meaning of the term. Trusting in. Relying upon. Clinging to. Giving one's self up to. And allowing Jesus to keep us.

Observe the tenses. They show a present and continuing process. One of total life commitment. To the person of Jesus Christ. This process, fully entered into, results in transformed lives. Without exception! It incorporates an exchange-life principle. Moment by moment. Choice by choice. We choose to exchange our self-serving thoughts and actions for those of Jesus. The *me*-centered mode will undergo a gradual replacement. By reaching out to others. Caring. Serving. Loving. There will no longer be room for hatred. Prejudice. Self-destructive behaviors. A critical spirit. Complaining. Always trying to get the best for ourselves.

The Bible message challenges every individual. To enter into a wholly new and life-changing friendship with God! A deeply personal relationship. Resulting in a transformation. Of the whole person. From the innermost depths of our being. Our most secret thoughts. Our deepest motives. Our wills. And our desires. The process can be slow and agonizing or it can be accelerated and rewarding. Depending on the choices we make in response to God's Word. Through our moment by moment obedience. As we learn to express God's value system. The rewards can be rich and deeply satisfying.

In summary, the act of becoming a Christian is simplicity itself. You are required to do nothing. Christ did it all. Simply talk to Jesus Christ. Tell him you are willing to let him turn your life around. Acknowledge the fact that you are a sinner. You have made bad choices. You need forgiveness. You will find it. Ask him to become your Savior and Lord. You will become a new person!

That's it! God accepted His Son's death on the cross. As complete payment for your sins. He died to take your "rap." And those of every living person in the world. Past! Present! And future! It's as simple as that. God will mysteriously impart the gift of His Holy Spirit. Into the innermost depths of your person. To enable you to live for Him. To set you free from whatever bondage has entrapped you. Welcoming you into a deeply personal friendship with the living, loving Creator God of the universe.

YOU WANT TO BECOME A CHRISTIAN BUT SOMEHOW FEEL YOU CAN'T

If you want to believe but simply feel you can't, remember that God appeals to your will. He made you! And your will! He also created and designed you to be His deeply personal friend. Don't forget the cosmic sting factor. Satan passionately desires to have you become a member of his tragic community. To be cut off from God. Forever! He doesn't want you to come to Christ. If you do he knows you'll be forever lost to his control. He can and will impart every imaginable reason. To block you from making this choice.

Listen to this invitation: "Come and let us reason together, saith the Lord; though your sins be as scarlet, they shall be as white as snow; though they be red like crimson, they shall be as wool."[25]

He also says, "O taste and see that the Lord is good! Happy is the man who takes refuge in him![26]

Find a quiet, private place. Now, simply talk to Jesus. Verbally! Tell him how you feel. Tell him of your doubts. Your burdens. Your hang-ups. Your loneliness. Your anger. Your frustration. Your disappointments. Tell him that if he is real, if he is who he says he is, you want him to enter your life. To give you his gift of eternal life. To live in your heart. To lift your burdens. To bring you peace. Continue these sessions daily. You will soon discover the reality of the unmeasurable. You will discover a new and heretofore unknown power. To deal with all of your deepest needs. In your private world. He will become utterly real to you. He will change your life. For the better.

Do not expect an overwhelming emotional experience. Your experience may vary greatly from those of others who have made this decision. Some have little or no feeling whatsoever. Others have a tremendously moving experience. If you feel nothing, it's easy to think, "It didn't work." That Christ did not give you the gift of eternal life as he promised. You must discount these feelings. That's what Satan wants you to believe. His sting operation is most effective at this point. His deception will attempt to deny the promises of Jesus Christ in your thought processes.

You must absolutely depend on the Word of God now! Implicitly! Completely! Totally! Unequivocally! Some individuals may be blessed with a sweet rush of tears. An unspeakable sense of purity and cleansing. Even of spontaneous prayer. Regardless of whether you feel these kinds of self-endorsing emotions or nothing whatsoever, believe God. If you were entirely sincere, you are now a child of God. You have the gift of eternal life. You have God's Holy Spirit living within you. Bank on it! It is truth!

Chapter Eleven
After Becoming a Christian

Shortly following the initial conversion experience, it is quite common for new believers to be assailed by doubt and uncertainty regarding the authenticity of their experience. Thoughts like "That was too easy," or "Am I just kidding myself about this? Just 'cause I want to go to heaven when I die?" "Does God really exist?" "I can't see or hear Him, so how can I really be sure?"

These kinds of doubts can become especially painful. As a result of the new believer failing to live up to a level of high performance—a level that is perceived necessary to stay on God's good side. An impossible standard is often erected in the mind of the new believer. When it is not consistently met, doubts and self-accusations come pouring into one's head. These feelings tend to cast doubt and overwhelm the entire commitment.

New, young converts are prime targets for Satan's accusative, undermining approach. Some even become so discouraged and guilt-ridden, they simply decide to give up. As a result of the artificial standard they have erected in their minds they even may soon come to feel that Christianity was merely a sham. Those who have fallen into this category are often the most difficult to restore to a relationship with God. They feel they have tried it. And it failed them. Why try again? Simply to face more guilt and failure?

The problem is not the failure of the faith. It's the failure of the individual to follow through in the pursuit of God. Every relationship, even on a purely human level, requires nurturing. This relationship much more so. It's a relationship that involves a total daily experience. A new personal world. A world now inhabited by God. In the person of His Son Jesus Christ.

To be enabled by God's Holy Spirit to face every obstacle life can hand you is necessarily time consuming. But tremendously rewarding! One cannot merely sit back and say, "Feed me," like a baby bird. God gave us His Word as the basis of our daily spiritual sustenance. Jesus said: "Man shall not live by bread alone, but by every word that proceeds from the mouth of God."[1]

Even as our physical body needs daily food and water for the maintenance of physical health, so our spiritual counterpart needs to be fed with the spiritual life-sustaining power of God's Word. Daily! We must learn to feed ourselves from God's book. By submitting to the teaching authority of God's Holy Spirit. He is the one Jesus described as, "The Spirit of truth who will guide us into all truth."[2]

The new Christian also needs to be involved regularly in group worship. A local church body. One which faithfully teaches God's Word. Supplying us with growth opportunities. To challenge, convict, and motivate us. To become accountable to God and to other Christians.

Another source of growth is the small group. These small group settings should have an atmosphere of loving acceptance. Of mutual identification with the stressful problems daily life assaults us with. These groups include an arena where members can bring their trials out into the open. Sharing without fear of rejection in order to deal with them from God's Word. To enlist the love, support, and understanding of others who face the same problems.

In some cases, problems may be too deeply personal even for a small group setting. Here is where one-on-one relationships can be valuable. Seek out a mature believer. Get together regularly. Be open and honest. Sometimes professional counseling is necessary. Seek out a good Christian counselor. Avoid non-believing counselors. They are not equipped to present Biblical counseling.

Preoccupation with past failures or tragedies can be an undermining influence. They can block spiritual growth. They turn our thoughts to self and frustrate God's gifts of love, joy, and peace. Gifts that should be the norm for our daily lives. We need to recognize once and for all the destructive nature of guilt. Then set it aside. The conscience will become greatly sensitized after having received God's Holy Spirit who indwells every believer. We must appropriate the fact that Jesus Christ paid the full penalty for our sins. Past. Present. And future. We need quickly to confess our wrong choices and fully forsake our guilt as we accept his full forgiveness. Then move on to the new challenges God has for us.

Remember. Guilt is one of Satan's best weapons against the new believer. Guilt can be the result of undisciplined thought lives. It's easy to fall into the trap of allowing negatives to rule our thought lives. We let our emotions run the gamut. From depression to discouragement. From lust to materialism. Negative memories of childhood. Parents. Siblings. From verbal abuse to physical abuse.

Satan can use these thoughts to hold us hostage to misery. To bondage. To a spiritually declining walk with God. This could be described as the emotional roller coaster syndrome. Satan delights in launching this entire spectrum of self-destructive thinking. To neutralize the joys of being a Christian. Of knowing God as a loving friend. Don't allow a negative thought life to undermine your relationship with God.

Satan would have us believe that we have no control over these negative emotions. Rather like being on a fast-moving express train. One we can't stop! A train that takes us wherever it's going, leaving us no choice as to its destination. We must recognize this new reality. As Christians, we have tapped into an entirely new power source. God's infinitely powerful spiritual resources. Resources with life-changing power. We will all be faced with a whole spectrum of negative emotions. Now, however, we are empowered by God's Holy Spirit! Enabling us to institute the exchange-life principle.

By exercising our faith we are to put off the old destructive nature and to put on Jesus Christ who is the source of our new nature.[3] We have a choice. We can either choose to live in bondage to our destructive thought patterns, or we can let the life of Christ flow through our lives. With his consequent love. Joy. And peace.

The practical application works like this. First we must ask God to make us sensitive to our thought patterns. To help us monitor our self-talk for its quality. Whether constructive or destructive. We must want God's goodness to flow through our lives. Some of our fantasies can be very compelling. Rewarding, but in a destructive way. The moment these thoughts occur, if we really desire to be the Lord's person, we can simply say to ourselves, "Help me, Jesus." This seemingly insignificant response is an exercise of faith. It will release God's power. Immediately! This process is succinctly expressed by the apostle Paul. He states: "To set the mind on the flesh is death, but to set the mind on the Spirit is life and peace."[4] You will be both amazed and delighted to see your thought patterns becoming more and more righteous as your level of joy increases.

The Christian life involves a continual ebb and flow in the process of developing our relationship with God. There will inevitably be times of doubt. Uncertainty. Discouragement. Disappointment with our performance spiritually. As we develop our friendship with God, our spiritual growth will result in a lessening of these "down" times. And they will have a decreasing influence over our thought lives. The times of delighting in our Savior will become increasingly sweet and precious. Indescribably so as we learn more and more of the wondrous loveliness of God's person.

He will become our inseparable, loving friend. Loving us without conditions. Through the active, dynamic exercise of our faith. Bringing the life of Jesus Christ into our everyday personal world. Thought by thought. Remember. Our free will gives us the privilege of deciding what to think. The way we choose to discipline our thought lives will decide the quality of our lives. Right choices in our thought lives will result in rewarding living. God will impact every department of our lives. Dramatically. And every detail of our daily conduct. Jesus Christ will become the supreme joy of our inner personal world.

PREOCCUPATION WITH SATAN

The nature of Satan's cosmic sting is world-wide. Invisible. Pervasive. And deceitful. The Bible says that Satan is the deceiver of the whole world.[5] Some Christians have severely retarded their spiritual growth by becoming too preoccupied with Satan. Our focus is to be upon Jesus Christ. Not on Satan. As Christians, we have been given victory over Satan. The only power he can have in our lives is delegated power. Delegated by us. When we fail to walk by faith, when we consciously permit sin to rule our lives, we become servants of the one whom we choose to obey.[6] Self and Satan. Or God. Serving Satan is a hard road to travel. It's filled with self-delusion and fantasy. Leaving one with emptiness. Spiritual bankruptcy. Serving God is the road to love, joy, and peace!

God has given every individual Christian an unlimited potential. We can be just as spiritual as we choose to be. We need to be aware of the fact that spiritual growth sometimes proceeds by trials. Painful trials.[7] The nature of faith is such that it must be continually stretched. And exercised. It has a powerfully self-endorsing aspect. Endorsing the truth of Christ in us.

As we apply faith to our daily trials, we see God's mysterious power released into our everyday circumstances. No matter how difficult they may be. Sometimes God's answers are slow in coming from our standpoint. But God's power has no limitations. It is more than abundant for every trial life can hand us. This is all a part of His program for our growth. To learn to trust Him. In every aspect of our lives.

We need to remember that we are in God's hands now. His children. The objects of His unceasing, unconditional love.[8]

You have an unspeakably tender, loving Heavenly Father inviting you into a life-revolutionizing relationship with Him.

He knows what it takes to fulfill your life. He created the universe. And He created you! To love and enjoy Him forever! You have a free choice. He loves you far too much ever to violate your will. Enter into His Kingdom, and rejoice throughout eternity.

"And this is life eternal, that they might know thee the only true God, and Jesus Christ, whom thou hast sent."[9]

Footnotes

Footnotes are from the New Scofield reference
Bible except where otherwise noted

Chapter 3
The Cosmic Sting

1. Luk. 8:14–15
2. Matt. 7:13–14
3. Eph. 2:2
4. Eph. 2:2
5. Eph. 6:12
6. Eph. 6:12
7. Eph. 6:12
8. II Cor. 10:5
9. II Cor. 4:4
10. Heb. 2:14
11. Jn. 12:31
12. Rev. 20:10
13. Matt. 12:24
14. Matt. 13:38
15. I Thes. 3:5
16. Jn. 8:44

17. Jn. 8:44
18. Matt. 13:39
19. II Cor. 11:14–15

Chapter 4
The Blinding Process

1. II Cor. 4:3–4
2. Prov. 5:21
3. Luk. 13:11–17
4. Mk. 9:14–29
5. Luk. 8:2
6. Acts 5:3
7. Matt. 16:23
8. Matt. 26:75
9. Jn. 13:2
10. Jn. 11:25

Chapter 5
Satan's Methodology

1. Prov. 14:12
2. Luk. 12:54–57
3. II Cor. 11:14
4. Gal. 6:7–8
5. I Cor. 3:18–19 (TLB)

Chapter 6
The Book of Truth

1. II Pet. 1:21
2. Deut. 11:32
3. Ex. 34:6
4. Ps. 33:4
5. Ps. 60:13

6. Ps. 100:5
7. Ps. 117:2
8. Ps. 119:42
9. Ps. 119:151
10. Ps. 146:6
11. Isa. 65:16
12. Jn. 14:6
13. Jn. 8:45
14. Jn. 17:17
15. Jn. 18:37
16. Rom. 2:2
17. II Cor. 6:7
18. Gal. 2:14
19. I Tim. 3:15
20. Jas. 1:18
21. Isa. 42:9
22. Isa. 43:5–9 (TLB)

Chapter 7
The Impact of Dimensional Truth

1. Prov. 6:16–19 (TLB)
2. Rom. 12:19
3. Jn. 15:12
4. Prov. 5:21–23

Chapter 8
Scientific Verification

1. Job 36:26–28
2. Eccl. 1:7
3. Isa. 40:22
4. Job 26:7
5. Ps. 102:5–6
6. Ps. 8:8

7. Lev. 17:11
8. Heb. 11:3
9. Eccl. 1:6
10. Ps. 139:16

Chapter 9
The Man of Truth

1. Isa. 7:14
2. Luk. 1:26–27
3. Mic. 5:12
4. Luk. 2:4–6
5. Num. 24:7–8; Hos. 11:1
6. Matt. 2:14–15
7. Mal. 3:1; Isa. 40:3–5
8. Matt. 3:1–3
9. Zech. 9:9
10. Matt. 25:6–11
11. Isa. 53:3–5; Ps. 69:7–8
12. Matt. 27:1–2
13. Zech. 11:12
14. Matt. 26:14–15
15. Ps. 22
16. Matt. 27:46–50
17. Ps. 69:21
18. Matt. 27:33–34
19. Ps. 22:16
20. Mk. 15:24
21. Ps. 22:18
22. Jn. 19:23–34
23. Ps. 34:19–20
24. Jn. 19:32–33
25. Ps. 16:9–10
26. Jn. 21:12, 14
27. Jn. 14:6
28. Jn. 10:30

29. Jn. 11:25–26
30. II Cor. 5:8
31. Matt. 26:63–66
32. Jn. 18:37
33. Jn. 16:33
34. Jn. 16:24
35. I Cor. 15:3–8
36. Mk. 8:31
37. Jn. 2:19–22
38. II Cor. 5:17 (RSV)
39. Jn. 4:25–26

Chapter 10
Becoming a Christian

1. Jn. 1:3
2. Jn. 3:16 (TLB)
3. Jn. 4:14 (RSV)
4. Jn. 5:24 (RSV)
5. Jn. 6:51 (RSV)
6. Jn. 8:12 (RSV)
7. Jn. 10:9 (RSV)
8. Jn. 11:25–26 (RSV)
9. Jn. 14:6 (RSV)
10. Jn. 16:24 (RSV)
11. Jn. 16:33 (RSV)
12. Jn. 17:3 (RSV)
13. Jn. 18:37 (RSV)
14. Rom. 3:23 (RSV)
15. Jn. 3:18
16. Ex. 20 (RSV)
17. I Jn. 3:15
18. Matt. 5:21–22
19. Eph. 5:5
20. Matt. 5:27–28
21. Rom. 7:19-21 (TLB)

22. II Cor. 5:19–21 (TLB)
23. Isa. 7:14
24. Heb. 11:1
25. Isa. 1:18
26. Ps. 34:8 (RSV)

Chapter 11
After Becoming a Christian

1. Matt. 4:4
2. Jn. 16:13
3. Eph. 4:22–23
4. Rom. 8:6
5. Rev. 12:9
6. Rom. 6:16
7. Js. 1:2–3
8. Jer. 31:3
9. Jn. 17:3